Comments on other *Amazing Stories* from readers & reviewers

"*Tightly written volumes filled with lots of wit and humour about famous and infamous Canadians.*"
Eric Shackleton, *The Globe and Mail*

"*The heightened sense of drama and intrigue, combined with a good dose of human interest is what sets* Amazing Stories *apart.*"
Pamela Klaffke, *Calgary Herald*

"*This is popular history as it should be... For this price, buy two and give one to a friend.*"
Terry Cook, a reader from Ottawa, on **Rebel Women**

"*Glasner creates the moment of the explosion itself in graphic detail...she builds detail upon gruesome detail to create a convincingly authentic picture.*"
Peggy McKinnon, *The Sunday Herald,* on **The Halifax Explosion**

"*It was wonderful...I found I could not put it down. I was sorry when it was completed.*"
Dorothy F. from Manitoba on **Marie-Anne Lagimodière**

"*Stories are rich in description, and bristle with a clever, stylish realness.*"
Mark Weber, *Central Alberta Advisor,* on **Ghost Town Stories II**

"*A compelling read. Bertin...has selected only the most intriguing tales, which she narrates with a wealth of detail.*"
Joyce Glasner, *New Brunswick Reader,* on **Strange Events**

"*The resulting book is one readers will want to share with all the women in their lives.*"
Lynn Martel, *Rocky Mountain Outlook,* on **Women Explorers**

# RESCUES ON
# THE HIGH SEAS

# RESCUES ON THE HIGH SEAS

## Tales of Survival, Hope, and Bravery

**ADVENTURE**

## by Mark Chatham

PUBLISHED BY ALTITUDE PUBLISHING CANADA LTD.
1500 Railway Avenue, Canmore, Alberta T1W 1P6
www.altitudepublishing.com
1-800-957-6888

Extreme care has been taken to ensure that all information presented in
this book is accurate and up to date. Neither the author nor the
publisher can be held responsible for any errors.

| | |
|---|---|
| Publisher | Stephen Hutchings |
| Associate Publisher | Kara Turner |
| Series Editor | Jill Foran |
| Editor | Lee Craig |

We acknowledge the financial support of the Government
of Canada through the Book Publishing Industry Development
Program (BPIDP) for our publishing activities.

**Altitude GreenTree Program**
Altitude Publishing will plant twice as many trees as were used
in the manufacturing of this product.

**National Library of Canada Cataloguing in Publication Data**

Chatham, Mark
 Rescues on the high seas / Mark Chatham.

(Amazing stories)
ISBN 1-55439-003-6

1. Canadian Coast Guard. 2. Search and rescue operations--Canada.
I. Title. II. Series: Amazing stories (Canmore, Alta.)

VG55.C3C42 2005        363.28'6'0971        C2004-906267-0

An application for the trademark for Amazing Stories™
has been made and the registered trademark is pending.

Printed and bound in Canada by Friesens
2 4 6 8 9 7 5 3 1

For those who risk their all to save
in peril, souls upon the sea.

# Contents

# Prologue

*Deep into the shift, it was the "mudman" on the oil rig Vinland who first realized something was awry. Responsible for circulating mud into the gas well to control the pressure, he noticed an alarming amount of mud coming back up, and he couldn't control the flow. The rig was parked 16 kilometres northeast of Sable Island, and this particular test well had been difficult, giving "kicks" of back pressure when the drillers had hit a couple of small gas pockets, but they had always coped and were never in danger.*

*Earlier that day, the drillers had sealed the bottom of the well two kilometres below the seabed using a steel plug topped with concrete. The drillers had also circulated mud through the hole to equalize the pressure and hold the plug in place. Their efforts weren't enough. The extreme gas pressure punched the plug free and started a disastrous sequence of events, despite the drillers' frantic attempts to solve the problem.*

*The well now acted like a howitzer. The expanding gas shot the plug up the bore of the well like an artillery round. The oil rig and its crew of 76 were directly in the line of fire. Hitting the ocean floor, the plug ploughed along the flexible hose that connected the wellhead on the seabed to the rig. At exactly 10:02 p.m., the mass of mud and gas slammed into the drill floor of the rig with enough impact to tear the six-ton turntable from its moorings, jamming it half a metre above its normally seated position while gas vented and mud gushed into the cold night air. One spark and the rig could explode and burn to the waterline.*

# Chapter 1
# Blowout on the *Vinland*

The night of February 22, 1984, had been quiet in the radio room aboard the *Vinland*, a Norwegian-owned oil rig leased by Shell Canada. It was near 10 p.m. on the last shift of radio operator Peter Fraser's three-week stint. He was sitting with his feet up, reading a paperback and listening to the distress and calling frequencies in his headphones. Peter was looking forward to the next morning when he would fly home and see his fiancée.

Suddenly, and without warning, he heard three consecutive loud noises — BANG! CRASH! BOOM! — and the rig gave a slight bounce. Peter looked out the radio room porthole, expecting to see that some pipe had slipped from the crane's grasp and fallen to the deck. Instead, he gazed in horror as a viscous black cloud that he thought was smoke roiled upwards, obscuring his view of the derrick. He didn't realize at the time that this turbulent, writhing, black column was mud. The combined force of the mud, concrete plug, and gas had smashed into the rig. Now, natural gas and mud were shooting straight up, as though blasting from a fire hose, because of the extreme pressure below.

To Peter, it looked as though there had been an explosion. He turned on his MF/HF radios, grabbed some paper, and started to log the incident. "2202 AST: bang — crash — boom, black smoke." Keeping a log of events is a key function aboard ship. At this point, he still had no idea what had happened and assumed there must have been horrible casualties. He waited for a call from Joan Evans, the medic. If she was busy tending to the injured in the ship's infirmary, Captain Breviks would show up and have Peter arrange for a medical evacuation to Halifax, Nova Scotia, by helicopter. There was no word from anyone.

Peter heard the supply vessel *Claymore Sea* on the air and called its crew to tell them what had happened and that the *Vinland* might need their assistance. The radio operator assured him the *Claymore Sea* was on its way. Supply vessels are large, ocean-going tugs that constantly shuttle drill equipment and provisions to the rigs. They look like sea-going flatbed trucks, having a high superstructure forward and a low, flat afterdeck to store whatever provisions or equipment are needed at the rig. Aside from constantly shuttling supplies, a supply tug is always standing by in the vicinity of the rig in case of an emergency.

Despite the fact that help was on the way, Peter's anxiety began to swell because he could hear people running in the hallway. Someone shouted something that he couldn't make out. Then he was left in silence, except for one unusual sound. Although it was muted in the confines of the radio room, there was no mistaking the low rumble of rolling thunder from the jetting mud and gas. Peter felt the deck vibrate ominously beneath his feet.

The *Vinland* was a semisubmersible oil rig. It was kept afloat by two immense pontoons that could be flooded to raise or lower the rig to a depth that would keep it stable in rough seas. The *Vinland* would then be anchored in that position by two anchors apiece from each of the four corners of the rig. Peter had started working on the *Vinland* immediately upon leaving radio school in Saskatoon, Saskatchewan, in September 1982. He and his fiancée had moved to Quebec City, and after every three-week rotation on the rig, he would fly there to see her. Three relaxing weeks at home and then it was back to the rig.

Peter enjoyed his time on the *Vinland*: the food was excellent, and while the accommodations were small, they were comfortable and included a washroom and shower stall. He also enjoyed the work. "I found working on the rig usually pleasant and the people great," he recalls. "I made many friends and I never found myself regretting departure from Quebec for the rig, nor was I upset when, after the three-week stint on the rig, fog would roll in and the helicopters would stay in Halifax." His only complaint was that his cabin was under the helicopter deck, which was very loud.

Working 12-hour shifts, or "watches," seven days a week for the three weeks aboard the rig, Peter's job was to maintain and operate all radio communications. He tended and operated the short- (VHF), medium- (MF), and long- (HF) range frequencies, radio sets, and satellite communications, as well as listening to the VHF and MF distress and calling frequencies. Peter's duties included patching through phone calls for company officials and personal calls for the crew, as well as copying Coast Guard broadcasts of weather and navigational hazard information and taking weather observations. It could be very busy at times, but it wasn't stressful work, and during slow periods he could take time to read. But there would be no more reading that night of February 22.

Jon Otterskred, the Norwegian off-duty radio operator, burst wide-eyed into the radio room, wearing his survival suit. Many of the ship's officers were Norwegian. The rest of the 76 crew members were Canadian. Jon asked Peter what was going on. Peter told him what he had heard and seen thus far and informed him he had no idea what was happening yet. At this point, all those who were involved in drilling operations were elsewhere, assessing the damage and trying to control the situation. Jon then told Peter he had encountered Erik, a driller, in the hallway, coated in mud and looking frightened. Peter hoped he'd hear from the captain soon.

Captain Breviks, however, had his hands full on the bridge, where he had been finishing his day's work when the blowout occurred. Within two minutes, the Shell company foreman advised him that the *Vinland* was suffering a gas leak. The captain knew the rig needed to be abandoned. Fortunately, the crew had trained for it every week. With no helicopters available, he felt the best option was to use the cranes to lower the crew in personnel baskets to the *Seaforth Commander*, the standby supply tug. But first, he had to sound the alarm.

RING ... RING ... RING ... Peter entered the time in his log. "2207 AST: fire alarm." Peter sent Jon off to find the captain and tell him that the *Claymore Sea* was en route and also to see if he could discover what was happening.

Only five minutes had elapsed since the rig had been smashed by the force of the blowout, and confusion was rampant. Jon returned quickly to tell Peter the message had been passed on. The captain was on the bridge talking frantically to a number of people on the phone and to the *Seaforth Commander* on the handheld VHF set. Once the fire alarm sounded, the response of the off-duty crew was immediate. Those who were sleeping awoke with a start and were galvanized to action. Everyone donned their survival suits and rushed to their emergency stations.

Survival suits are a necessity for sailors in the Atlantic Ocean. The waters of the Atlantic are intensely cold in winter

— cold enough that a person who ends up in the water can drown almost immediately from a physiological phenomenon called "cold shock," which is an involuntary response to freezing water that makes one gasp for air. If cold shock doesn't kill the unfortunate victim, hypothermia will. Survival suits are waterproof, orange, neoprene rubber suits that keep sailors sufficiently dry and warm in order for them to live long enough for help to arrive. The air inside the suits also provides enough buoyancy to keep a person afloat. Sailors often call these suits "Gumby suits" — when they're wearing them they look like orange versions of the Gumby character from the old television show. On the *Vinland*, the crew had two suits for every man aboard.

Before Peter could get his survival suit on, the power died, leaving him and Jon sitting nervously in the dark. Peter flipped on the emergency light and dutifully wrote in his log: "2214: power failure."

The *Vinland* was now operating exclusively on its emergency battery power supply, which provided emergency lighting and power to the radios. Having only emergency power meant the cranes could not function; using them to evacuate was out of the question. The crew would have to evacuate by lifeboat, instead. This change of plans, however, could not be announced over the now-powerless public address system. Instead, crew members were informed of the new evacuation plans by word of mouth, which only increased the confusion.

Abandoning the rig would be a dangerous undertaking. The following had to happen: crew members had to make their way in the dark to their lifeboat stations; without adequate lighting, they had to cross decks slick with muck; after boarding the lifeboats, they had to be lowered 21 metres to the ocean's surface; once away from the rig, they had to get out of the lifeboat and onboard one of the supply vessels. This last part was particularly treacherous — the danger of falling overboard and being crushed between the life capsule and the hull of the ship was very real, as was the danger of capsizing the lifeboat.

Dave Lever, the second mate and navigation officer on the *Claymore Sea*, was sleeping when the chief engineer burst into his room to wake him an hour before his midnight to 6 a.m. night watch. Unlike on an oil rig, when a ship is at sea, shifts are in a continuous cycle of six hours on, six hours off. Sleep is always at a premium.

"Dave! We need you on the bridge! The rig is having a problem and is being abandoned." Without another word, the chief engineer hurried off to rouse the rest of the crew.

Abandoned! The word was a mental light switch, snapping Dave from the twilight of awakening to instant and full alertness. If the rig was being abandoned, the problem had to be very serious indeed. Throwing on his work clothes, he quickly made his way to the bridge.

If the ship's engine room, with the engines, circulating pumps, generators, and all the machinery that provides a ship's muscle, is the heart of a vessel, then the bridge is certainly its brain. It's the command centre where the captain and officers exert control. They steer, navigate, control the ship's speed and power, and act as the ship's eyes both by maintaining a visual lookout and using radar. The bridge is also the ship's ears and voice because the radio operators send and receive messages on various radio frequencies: ship to ship, company frequencies, and, most importantly, distress frequencies.

It was shortly after 11 p.m. when Dave arrived on the bridge, which was lit only by the soft glow of the instruments. The radio frequencies were alive with a much higher volume of radio traffic than normal. There were two other people on the bridge. Captain Keith Gear was working the aft wheelhouse controls, manoeuvring with bow thrusters and engines. Also on the bridge was the chief engineer. He would operate pumps, winches, and searchlights from the bridge during the rescue. Meanwhile, on deck, First Mate Mike Pym and the entire crew of 12 were making preparations for the rescue.

Dave took his own place at the chart table. It was his job to monitor and work the radios, plot the positions on the charts, and check the weather forecasts. It was also his job to advise Captain Gear of any problems that may arise based on what he was seeing on the charts and from what he was reading in the weather reports. There are shoals off Sable Island, and Dave needed to advise the captain on a course of action to avoid them.

# Blowout on the Vinland

Dave now learned the true extent of the danger. The *Vinland* had suffered a catastrophic blowout that had natural gas spewing hundreds of metres into the air and downwind from the rig. One spark would incinerate the rig and everything around it, including any vessels that were close by attempting to rescue those aboard the oil rig.

The *Claymore Sea* poured on maximum speed, punching over three-metre waves in an explosion of froth to arrive as quickly as possible at the rescue site. It would be there in half an hour. Tension and anxiety suffused the crew as the ship drew closer to the cloud of gas that could burn them all to death if it ignited. Although special mesh covered the smokestacks of all supply vessels so that no spark could escape to ignite the gas, it was small consolation when there were so many other uncontrollable factors that could create the conflagration they all feared. What drove them on was the knowledge there were people on the rig who needed their immediate help. Only the supply vessels in the area were close enough to help the crew of the *Vinland* survive this catastrophe.

As the *Claymore Sea* drew closer to the *Vinland*, the chief engineer turned to Dave and said somberly, "It looks like a death's-head on the water."

Looking in the direction of the rig, Dave realized he was right. The power was out, and only a few emergency lights provided light on the rig, which was still spewing mud high into the night air. The *Vinland* looked like a ghastly and hideous skull from which smoke was pouring. The eerie rumbling sound that the over-pressurized gas made as it shot up only deepened Dave's unease.

## Coping with Confusion

Meanwhile, on the *Vinland*, the Shell company representative entered the radio room to make an urgent call to headquarters in Dartmouth, Nova Scotia. Peter Fraser patched him through by using a company frequency on the MF radio. He got through right away, and while handing the handset to the Shell executive, he noticed both Jon and the Shell man were wearing survival suits. "It occurred to me that I'd better get mine on now, because for all I knew I may not have time to do so later," recalls Peter.

While putting on his survival suit, Peter could hear the Shell representative telling the person on the other end of the line to alert the helicopter company to prepare to evacuate the rig because they'd suffered a partial blowout. Peter now felt somewhat optimistic. After all, it was only a *partial* blowout. Helicopters were coming to evacuate them. There was a lot of rumbling but no fire, so he assumed they were safe for now. The Shell representative finished his call and left the room.

Jon's face held an expression of shock as he blurted out, "Wow, a blowout! Goodness. That's bad! That's why Erik was covered in mud."

Captain Breviks opened the door to the radio room and

told Peter to advise the Rescue Coordination Centre (RCC) in Halifax of the situation. "Okay, Captain," Peter replied, and then the captain was gone. Peter dialled up 2182, the MF international distress and calling frequency on the radio, to call Halifax Coast Guard Radio. Halifax was too far away to use the shorter-range VHF frequencies.

It was around 10:20 p.m., and Scott Clements had about an hour and a half left in his evening shift at Halifax Coast Guard Radio when the call came through on 2182 from the *Vinland*. Scott instructed Peter to switch to a working channel, which was the only way a phone patch could be made by radio. Scott assumed that the *Vinland* wanted to make a routine phone call to its agent, or perhaps one of the crew was making a phone call home — workers often got homesick during their three-week stretch on the rig. But Peter's next words set alarm bells off in Scott's head. "Halifax, *Vinland*. We need to place a phone call to the Rescue Coordination Centre."

A call to the RCC could be for any number of things, none of them good as far as Scott was concerned. His anxiety increased, but he placed a phone call to the duty officer at RCC and patched him through to the rig. Scott monitored the call and heard Peter telling the RCC coordinator that the *Vinland* had an unconfirmed blowout and that the crew likely needed to abandon the rig. From the tension in Peter's voice, Scott knew the rig was in serious trouble. He had been at his job for a year and a half and had never worked an emergency of this scale. If the rig declared a Mayday, it would be his first.

Peter passed along the basic information the RCC needed: the particulars of the rig, the type of emergency, and how many people were on board. He couldn't remember the rig's position; the Post-it Note containing this data, which was usually on the console, was missing. However, rig positions are monitored closely by the Coast Guard, and the RCC had the information it needed. Scott heard the RCC duty officer tell Peter to stand by and let the RCC know if there were any changes. Then the phone call was finished. Peter asked Scott to keep that frequency clear. The captain of the rig was the only individual who could formally declare a Mayday. Peter would have to wait until Captain Breviks gave the word before he could declare one. Peter wrote the time in his log: "2220: contact with RCC."

Aboard the *Vinland*, Jon Otterskred went to tell Captain Breviks that the RCC had been informed. Peter was left to monitor the radios. Jon returned a few minutes later, looking uncomfortable. "They're getting everyone to the boats, Peter," he said. "I should get going, unless you want me to stay?"

"No, no, you go ahead, I'll be alright ... but you'd better be back here at midnight!" replied Peter with a bit of humour to ease the tension — Jon would have relieved Peter at midnight had this been a normal night.

With Jon's departure, Peter was once again alone in the radio room. He switched over to channel 13, the working channel for the *Vinland*, and anxiously listened to the ongoing chatter as the crew prepared to abandon.

*Blowout on the* Vinland

With the power out and no public address system, word was still spreading slowly among the crew that they would be abandoning the rig by lifeboat. For some it wasn't clear whether they would be using the aft or forward lifeboats. A 25-knot wind was blowing mud toward the stern. Everything downwind and in the immediate vicinity of the oil derrick was coated in a thick layer of the slippery, slimy muck. Despite this, several crew members had struggled in the dark to the aft boat stations and were waiting for further orders, all the while under a thick rain of mud. The *Seaforth Commander* had made its way to the *Vinland's* stern, and its searchlight stroked a finger of light over the darkened rig, providing illumination for the crew gathering at the aft boat deck. Eventually, someone got word to those gathered that they would be using the forward lifeboats, which were upwind and out of the spray of mud and gas. Everyone began struggling their way forward.

While the crew gathered at the forward lifeboat stations, Joan Evans, the medic, took charge of the evacuation procedure that they had practised every Sunday. Joan had an evacuation list and checked off all the names as crew members entered the first lifeboat. She ensured they were wearing survival suits and that they were zipped up properly and ready to go. Boat number one was launched.

In the radio room, Peter's anxiety was growing. Then on the radio, he heard something that increased his unease to near panic level. A Norwegian voice was saying, "*Ja, leefbooten nummer en utgangen,*" and another voice was responding, "*Ja ja, det er bra.*" Peter recalls: "My last year and a half had taught me enough Norwegian to understand the exchange. 'Lifeboat number one is now leaving.' 'Okay, very good.' "

Boat number one was leaving without him! He grabbed the handset and called out, "Hey boys — don't forget your radio operator now!"

No response. Forcing himself to calm down, Peter pondered the situation and realized that only one lifeboat had been launched. The second lifeboat hadn't left yet. There were evacuation lists and procedures to be followed. He was on the list, so surely the crew wouldn't leave without him. Feeling assured, he stayed at the radio and awaited word from the captain or from the RCC.

After having been informed of the situation, the RCC sprang into action, assessing the situation and making preparations to coordinate the rescue in anticipation of the Mayday call from the rig. It alerted the rescue squadron at Shearwater airbase in Dartmouth to get a couple of helicopters ready to assist. It also called the airbase in Summerside, Prince Edward Island, ordering that two Voyageur helicopters and the twin engine Buffalo aircraft be made ready to head to the area.

Meanwhile, Scott Clements called Peter and asked him about the weather conditions, which would affect the aircraft. Peter told him that the wind was blowing from the northwest at 25 knots, and that the seas were around three metres. The skies were clear for the moment, but the weather was going to worsen. Scott dutifully passed the information to the RCC. While Peter sat back to await word from the bridge, he looked out the porthole and could still see wispy, steam-like smoke billowing from the area of the derrick. Captain Breviks poked his head into the radio room and told Peter to tell the RCC that the platform was to be abandoned. It was time to send a Mayday. Peter called Halifax Coast Guard Radio.

Still waiting and listening to the working frequency, Scott couldn't help but ponder how different the unfolding emergency was from the "by-the-book," cookie-cutter distress exercises he had worked at the Coast Guard College. In those scenarios everything was neat and tidy and followed procedures precisely. The *Vinland* situation was unlike anything he'd experienced at the college. Still, it was an *unconfirmed* blowout, so it could be a false alarm. Then Scott heard three words on the working frequency that confirmed his worst fears: "Halifax, *Vinland.* Mayday."

These three simple words sent Scott's adrenal gland into overdrive. When a radio operator hears the word "Mayday," the effect is electric and immediate. Scott was well aware that he was the communications lifeline for those in mortal danger; it was imperative that he do the best job possible to help save lives. He replied immediately, "*Vinland*, Halifax. Go ahead your message, over."

"Halifax, *Vinland.* Mayday. Time 230237UTC. We are abandoning the platform in two orange-coloured, 50-man enclosed lifeboats. No injuries reported, 76 persons on board, weather is like I passed to you earlier, no fire yet. *Seaforth Commander* should be on scene with *Claymore Sea* en route not far away. We are abandoning at this time."

Scott got some additional information about the lifeboats and the number of people aboard them, then said, "Roger, *Vinland*. Received your Mayday. I will inform RCC. I suggest you retransmit your distress on 2182." The channel they were presently on was a working frequency — nobody else had heard Peter's Mayday. Scott advised Peter to retransmit it on the distress frequency, which everyone was required by law to monitor.

"Roger. I'll do that, thanks," Peter said.

"Okay. Good luck. I'll see you when you get ashore."

"Yeah, see you in a few hours."

That was the last time Scott spoke directly to Peter. Scott then began logging all that had transpired and copied the Mayday transmission as Peter made it on 2182.

Every ship that hears a Mayday is supposed to alter course and head to the position of the distress immediately. The crews also call the person sending the distress message, acknowledge that they heard it, and give an estimated time of arrival (ETA) to the position. A number of ships responded to Peter's call, including St. John's Coast Guard Radio. Peter was in the midst of answering another call when Captain Breviks arrived.

"Okay, Peter, we're going now."

"Just got to give ..."

"Now."

There was no arguing with the captain. Peter dropped the microphone and followed him into the darkened hallway. Lighting the way with a flashlight, the captain headed toward the bridge with Peter following closely. They were the last to leave.

They wound their way through passageways, across the bridge, and through the door to the steps leading to the forward boat deck and salvation. As they arrived at the top of the stairs, the *Seaforth Commander* was charging into view in an explosion of spray on the starboard side of the rig, an impressive sight that left Peter awestruck. Searchlights from the *Seaforth Commander* probed ahead, locking onto lifeboat number one and pinning the lifeboat to the water to keep it in sight.

The captain and Peter clambered down the ladder to the boat deck, where the locker holding the survival suits stood open. Some of the suits still hung in the locker, while others were scattered about the deck. The crew had removed their shoes and boots to get into the survival suits, and these, too, were strewn about — although some were placed neatly side by side as though awaiting the return of their owners.

Arriving at the lifeboat, Peter and the captain were greeted by Joan, who was standing under the dim glow of the emergency lights by the open lifeboat hatch. She was holding the clipboard that contained the evacuation list. The training and drills the crew had undergone every week had paid off handsomely. Peter hadn't been forgotten and left behind on the platform, a fact for which he was grateful.

Captain Breviks felt he should take one last look around before the lifeboat launched. He turned to leave and then stopped. Facing Peter and Joan, he said, "Don't leave without me."

"Oh no," replied Joan. "I'm not moving from this spot until you get back."

The captain nodded and disappeared into the darkness for one last sweep of the rig while Peter climbed into the lifeboat.

After Peter had left the radio, Scott Clements took over coordinating communications. He logged the ships that responded with their positions and ETAs to the distress position and passed the information on to the RCC, which would chart all the vessels that had responded. Some of the vessels were told they would be taking part in the subsequent rescue operations, while others were told to continue on with their journeys because they were too far away to be of assistance.

At the end of his shift, Scott was relieved of duty. He wasn't able to sleep for hours because he spent much of the time pondering all that had happened and hoping that everything went well for the crew of the *Vinland*.

The first thing Peter noticed on entering the lifeboat was that it held a lot of nervous people. Although they had performed boat drills every week and everyone was used to being in the lifeboat, this time it was for real. They would be launching and not returning. Many of the crew members were pale, and a few were covered in mud from working in the vicinity of the gushing flow of the well. Being careful not to tread on anyone, Peter had to work his way through the boat on his hands and knees. He was trying to get to a seat on the forward port side next to the lifeboat's radio. As it turned out, the seat had been saved for him, so he hunkered down between the lifeboat radio and one of the crane operators. One of the crew made a joke about this being a lousy way to do a crew change as Peter sat down and strapped himself in with the complicated seat belt. The three-fingered gloves of the survival suit made it cumbersome.

The lifeboat was totally enclosed; if it overturned in heavy seas it would right itself. It had an engine that was in a 1.4 x 1.4 metre fibreglass box, which was about a metre high and placed a metre from the back of the boat. Just behind the engine was a seat for the coxswain, the person who would steer the boat and work the controls for the engine and the VHF radio. The night of the blowout, Per Bygnes, one of the Norwegian crew members, was sitting in the coxswain's seat. His seat was raised high enough so that his feet could rest on the engine compartment. Per had three windows — forward, port, and starboard — to look out while he steered the little vessel to safety. Directly behind his head was the VHF radio.

Peter had just finished buckling in when Joan and Captain Breviks came down through the hatch into the lifeboat. Peter was nervous about the wind. Given the direction and force with which the wind was blowing, it was possible that the lifeboat could be blown back into the rig if the engine didn't catch. And there was a lot of metal under the platform that could smash the little fibreglass boat and sink it. The thought scared Peter so much that he ripped his gloves off and frantically tried to undo his seatbelt to give himself a chance to escape should this happen.

Meanwhile, Per Bygnes followed the launch procedures correctly. Three simple steps launched the lifeboat: charging the air lines to the two lifeboat hooks, pulling the release handle, and then releasing the brake handle. The boat would then start its descent to the water. The governor on the winch kept the descent smooth, steady, and not too fast. "Start the engine," someone called out. Per engaged the brake, leaving the boat hanging 12 metres in the air, in order to start the engine.

The lifeboat crew needed a running start when they hit the water. As the engine was punched to life it roared noisily within the confines of the boat. Per released the brake and once again they were dropping towards the ocean. As it turned out, hitting the water was unexpectedly gentle. The hooks fell free once the weight of the boat no longer held them in place. Peter was startled as the hooks banged and scraped along the side of the lifeboat. Motoring away from the rig was a roller coaster ride. At this point, the seas were running with three-metre swells, and the lifeboat was pitching up and down with every swell. Peter checked his watch; it was 11:10 p.m.

The lifeboat, which was constantly riding up the crest of one wave and then down into the trough of another, pulled away from the rig. Within five minutes, Peter was struck with seasickness. A wave of nausea hit him and he threw up. Someone else followed suit, and it wasn't long before the bouncy ride started taking its toll on others. Looking at his watch, Peter saw that it was 11:25 p.m. He vowed not to look at his watch again so long as he was in the boat. It was a vow he kept.

**Convoy**

The *Claymore Sea* had crept to within 200 metres of the rig and was illuminating the area with its searchlights when the second lifeboat launched. Together, the *Claymore Sea* and the *Seaforth Commander* had to guide the two lifeboats out to a safer area before the transfer of the boats' occupants could begin. The crews of both supply vessels were nervous and anxious to get out of the vicinity of the rig as quickly as possible, owing to the danger of explosion and fire.

The plume of gas from the *Vinland* hadn't yet ignited, and if this occurred, nobody wanted to be in the area to suffer the experience. It was spewing into the atmosphere unchecked, reaching 600 to 1,000 metres and curling downwind. The RCC had declared an aircraft exclusion zone up to 8,000 metres high within an eight-kilometre radius of the rig. A plane flying through the gas plume could inadvertently ignite it from the heat of its engines.

Aboard the *Claymore Sea*, Dave Lever could hear the rumbling of the blowout over the sound of the supply vessel's engines. These sounds, the wind and waves, and the sight of mud spewing from the rig magnified everyone's sense of dread. They were anxious to leave. The supply vessels locked on to the lifeboats with their searchlights and began guiding them out of the area.

The *Seaforth Commander* was followed by lifeboat number one. It would be the *Claymore Sea*'s responsibility to attend to lifeboat number two. Dave checked the weather reports and told Captain Gear that the weather and sea conditions were going to deteriorate. The wind was building, snow was falling, and the seas would eventually reach almost five metres — too rough to attempt to transfer the occupants of the boats. The visibility, already poor, was going to get worse, and snow squalls and sleet would make the rescue more complicated. The winds would be picking up to 40 knots, gale force, so it was decided that the crew of the *Claymore Sea* needed to transfer the lifeboat occupants quickly.

The captains of the supply vessels conferred. It was decided that the *Seaforth Commander* would be the on-scene commander, taking charge of coordinating the situation and the roles of the other vessels as they arrived. Two other ships, the *Trinity Bay* and the *Balder Hudson*, were on their way to the *Vinland*'s position. Both were supply vessels that were already in the oil field, and both would be arriving shortly.

Aboard the *Claymore Sea*, Dave breathed a sigh of relief once the second lifeboat started to separate from the *Vinland.* Now came the tricky part: getting the occupants of the lifeboats onto the ships. This manoeuvre was very difficult, not only because of the rough seas but because the coxswains driving the lifeboats didn't have much experience in small-boat handling, never mind operating them in such rough conditions.

The lifeboats were running parallel to the supply vessels, about 30 metres away, and were trying to work their way in closer. Limited visibility through the small windows of the lifeboats made it difficult. Another intimidating factor for the inexperienced coxswains was the seesaw effect of riding up one wave while a supply ship dropped down another. The lifeboats would drop into the trough of a wave and the coxswains would see the lights of the supply vessels looming high above them as the ships crested a wave, looking as though they would fall on top of the lifeboats and smash them to bits. Dave was hoping that the coxswain of lifeboat two would understand what the *Claymore Sea* wanted him to do — close at a steady but cautious rate so the two vessels would synchronize their motion as they got closer. If lifeboat two closed with the *Claymore Sea*, it would be riding the same wave as it neared, and the vessels would rise and fall together.

As the coxswains manoeuvred the small boats, many of

those watching couldn't help but think of the *Ocean Ranger* tragedy. Two years earlier, almost to the day, the semisubmersible drill rig *Ocean Ranger* had sunk in a huge storm off the Grand Banks in Newfoundland with the loss of all 84 crew. One lifeboat had gotten away but had capsized when those aboard had crowded to one side of the boat attempting to get aboard the ship rescuing them. The thought of the *Ocean Ranger* made the already apprehensive coxswains even more nervous to approach the supply vessels.

On the deck of the *Claymore Sea*, the first mate and crew were ready to attempt the rescue. When the lifeboat came alongside, two crew members wearing safety lines would be standing on tire fenders on the outer part of the hull. (The fenders are tractor tires that are hung on the outside of the hull to act as a buffer between the hull of the ship and the hull of a vessel the tug may be pushing. They also act as a buffer between the vessel and a pier where it may be tied up.) The rest of the crew stood behind, waiting to receive the lifeboat occupants two at a time. They had improvised a system where the survivors would be handed down to the galley for first aid and warming if necessary. The ship could handle up to 80 people, having fold-up cots and a ready supply of blankets and sheets. Prior to this, several safety lines had to be rigged and a small Zodiac aboard had to be prepared to launch in case someone fell into the water and had to be pulled out. For 40 minutes, the *Claymore Sea*'s crew tried to coax the lifeboats in closer, but they couldn't manage to bring them alongside. They had to come up with another plan.

The captains of the *Claymore Sea* and *Seaforth Commander* once again conferred and decided they wouldn't be able to affect a rescue until dawn. Checking the charts, Dave gave Captain Gear all the information he had on the shoals around Sable Island. Discussing this information with Dave, Captain Gear felt that the most sensible approach would be to form a small convoy and guide the lifeboats to the lee of Sable Island and perhaps even beach the lifeboats there. Because of the dangerous shoals in the area, they decided beaching the lifeboats was too risky. However, they could bring the convoy close enough to Sable Island so that it would provide the two lifeboats with some shelter from the heavy seas, making it safer to evacuate the lifeboats. It would also be much safer to engage in the rescue in daylight.

After conferring with the captain of the *Seaforth Commander*, Dave called Halifax Coast Guard Radio to tell them the new plan, and the information was passed to RCC. It was a sensible idea, and RCC concurred with the decision. The coxswains of the lifeboats were called and advised of the plan and everyone got into position for the long night of sailing ahead.

Sable Island is a solitary, thin, 30-kilometre crescent of sand and grass that juts out of the Atlantic Ocean 300 kilometres east of Halifax. Long a hazard for ships crossing the Atlantic, it's known as the "Graveyard of the Atlantic," and its waters are laden with wrecked ships — over 350 of them. In the 1960s, oil and natural gas were discovered off Sable Island. With the energy crunch of the 1970s, it became viable to explore for oil and gas in a serious manner, and around Sable Island, oil rigs dot the ocean like frontier towns of the Old West.

It was around 1 a.m. when the little convoy formed to make its way to Sable Island, 16 kilometres away. It proceeded along in single file, with the *Seaforth Commander* in the lead, followed by lifeboat number one, and then the *Claymore Sea*, followed by lifeboat number two. Bringing up the rear was the *Trinity Sea*, which had by now arrived on scene. It was also around this time that the Buffalo, a powerful twin-engine transport plane, arrived from Summerside and began circling the area.

Aboard lifeboat two, almost everyone was feeling the effects of seasickness and the stench of vomit permeated the stuffy cabin. At one point the smell was so pungent that one of the crew opened the small forward hatch to allow fresh air to blow in, giving everyone a bit of relief. He couldn't keep it open for very long; however, it was near zero outside and it quickly became very cold inside the cabin. About a minute after it was opened, the hatch had to be closed.

One man aboard lifeboat two was especially chilly. He was too large to fit into the standard size survival suits and had a tailor-made survival suit ordered that hadn't yet arrived. Though he was wearing a fitted helicopter escape suit, it wasn't as warm as a survival suit. As he grew colder and colder, someone called for the blankets that were among the supplies aboard the lifeboat.

The problem was that the supplies were stored under the seats. Peter wanted to help, but seasickness had left him in a state of crippled torpor that felt like near death. He tried to convince the fellow sitting across from him to draw enough strength to move so Peter could check the bin. Eventually, the young man struggled free and flopped across an empty seat. The bins weren't marked. When Peter finally fought through the complicated process to open the seat and check the bin, he reached in to discover it contained flares rather than the blankets that were so sorely needed. Drained and lacking the strength to continue his search, he closed the bin and slumped back into his seat, leaving the task of finding the blankets to others.

The situation became more urgent when, at some point during the night, 30-year-old Bob Lamb suffered a stress-related heart attack. The medic struggled to help, but hampered by lack of equipment and the rough seas, there wasn't much she could do. An urgent call was made to the supply vessels. Bob needed immediate evacuation to a hospital, but in the pitch black of the stormy Atlantic night it was impossible. The crew hoped he could hang on for the few hours until daylight.

Aboard the *Claymore Sea*, Dave had his hands full. He was plotting the convoy's position on the chart, marking its course, and monitoring the constant chatter on the bridge radios. Dave was singing out the positions of the shoals to the captain, who was trying to maintain a good course and speed to keep lifeboat two in view. The chief engineer was operating the searchlight to keep the lifeboat pinned within its beam, which was becoming more and more difficult as the night progressed. By this time it had begun to snow, and the seas were becoming rougher. The lifeboat wasn't showing up on radar, and with no external lights, it was tough to keep it in sight. Every once in a while a sudden squall of snow would blow up, the lifeboat would drop into a trough, and the chief engineer would urgently sweep the light to and fro, attempting to pick the lifeboat out in the blackness of the night. If for some reason the lifeboat wasn't making good speed, the *Trinity Sea* could potentially run it over, so it was crucial that the supply vessel keep it in sight. It was also bad for the crew members who were maintaining a lookout on the deck. Half of those involved in the earlier preparations were spelled so they could catch some sleep; the other half were kept ready to respond to an emergency immediately and were working in miserable conditions to keep the lifeboat in sight.

"It was very cold, and wet snow conditions were bad on deck. All our guys wore Mustang Floater suits. Not many could sleep knowing we had 33 people in a boat so close and yet we were unable to do anything to help them," Dave recalls.

As the situation stood, the crew was making reasonable

progress, bow on to the waves. If the engines quit, the small craft would eventually be pushed side on to the building swells and could very well end up rolling. So far, however, everyone's luck seemed to be holding out. Dave hunkered over the chart table and stayed focused on the job he had to do. There was a lot of chatter on the radio, and at one point on the company frequency someone wanted to know the condition of the oil rig. It was the last thing Dave cared about at this point. He and his crewmates were intent on saving the lives of those in the lifeboats, and now it appeared as though one of them was having a heart attack.

Through the night, rescue helicopters arrived, but owing to the deplorable weather conditions, as well as the danger from the gas downwind from the rig, they were shunted to other places to wait until dawn. Three of them went one each to the three drilling rigs in the area, the *Bow Drill 1*, the *Zapata Scotian*, and the *Sedco 709*, while the final helicopter put down on Sable Island for the night to wait out the weather, which was expected to calm by morning. It would be up to the supply vessels to guide the lifeboats to safe haven and get the occupants aboard. Until then, those aboard the lifeboats would have to ride it out.

Peter was as sick as he had ever been in his life. The seasickness came in bouts, starting with a slowly escalating feeling of nausea that eventually erupted in gut-wrenching retching. Then he would have a few blissful minutes of serenity before the cycle would repeat itself, over and over again. It was the same for many in both boats. Eventually, Peter's stomach calmed and he fell mercifully asleep. When he awoke, he realized that he was feeling better, the boat wasn't riding so hard, and people were talking. He also realized that daylight was filtering in, and their ordeal would soon be over.

The seas had died down enough for the coxswains to work their way in and snuggle up to the supply vessels. Inside lifeboat two, the middle hatch opened up. Peter could see blue sky and feel fresh air blowing in. Everyone had unbuckled their seat belts and was crowding around the hatch, anxious to get out. Up until then it had been an orderly scene, but it seemed that once the hatch opened, an air of urgent tension had come with it. Peter recalls: "We were alongside the supply boat and I could see people jumping across from the top of the boat to the supply boat — maybe a metre and a half gap — with the lifeboat and supply boat bobbing about quite a bit. I worried that if we slid up a little too close to the supply boat when she was coming down we could be rolled right under. The last place I wanted to be when that happened was in the midst of the mob trying to get out of that hatch."

He waited back by the smaller forward hatch, figuring that would be his escape route if anything happened. He wasn't sure if he was being overly paranoid about the situation, but after making it through all that had happened and with salvation in sight, he didn't want to take any chances.

Eventually, only a few people were left. Peter made his way to the central hatch to leave the lifeboat. "The sun was just up in the east, barely above the water, and a brilliant gold was glittering off the waves," he remembers. "Planes! Helicopters! Boats! Ships! Wow! Off to the east was the other lifeboat and its supply boat picking them up. A search-and-rescue Buffalo roared past overhead, another circled high in the sky. A Labrador helicopter was slowly chopping its way in to the *Claymore Sea*, a couple of Zodiacs were zipping around ready to pick anyone out of the water if need be. Absolutely marvellous! Fantastic!"

The rescue procedure that had been prepared aboard the *Claymore Sea* went fluidly and without a hitch. There were scramble nets slung over the side of the ship. The two crewmen standing on the fenders caught the lifeboat occupants as they stepped across and grabbed onto the scramble nets, assisting them in getting aboard the supply tug. Making the step across to the *Claymore Sea*, Peter felt grateful to finally be off the lifeboat. He was standing on the deck talking with another of the crew when he saw the stretcher carrying Bob Lamb. The Labrador helicopter that had been heading toward the *Claymore Sea* hovered overhead and lowered a search-and-rescue technician to prepare to lift the stretcher and evacuate Bob to Halifax. Once everything was ready, the stretcher was winched into the helicopter, and the helicopter departed. Sadly, Bob Lamb was pronounced dead on arrival at the hospital in Halifax.

After the Labrador had flown off, Peter went below to the mess, where the cook had coffee and hot chocolate for everyone. Many just wanted to find a bunk and sleep, but those who stayed up were very talkative and relived their ordeal in detail. The crew on the *Claymore Sea* did what they could to make the others feel comfortable. Many crewmen loaned spare clothing to those from the *Vinland* so they could wash their own soiled attire. The lifeboat was then taken in tow, and the supply vessel was once again making way, this time for the nearby oil rigs.

The *Claymore Sea* made its way to the *Zapata Scotian*, where the *Vinland* crew was taken aboard to await evacuation to Halifax by helicopter. After the crew was flown to Halifax, Shell put them up in nice hotels, paid for their meals, and bought them clothes to replace those that had been ruined during the ordeal. However, the first thing Peter did was to call his fiancée in Quebec City to let her know that all was well.

The blowout lasted for nine days. On March 3, a helicopter flew in from the windward side and gingerly hovered close over the *Vinland*'s deck. Three technicians hopped out and went aboard, and the helicopter flew off again. The technicians managed to restart the *Vinland*'s engines and provide power so they could begin the task of shutting down the flow of gas from the well. With the *Balder Husum* and *Bonavista Bay* assisting by pumping mud to the rig, the technicians contained the uncontrolled venting gas and killed the blowout within 24 hours. Eventually, the *Vinland* was once again put back in service.

## Chapter 2
# The Last Voyage of the *Rowan Gorilla 1*

**E**veryone was relaxed as they began the voyage shortly after 8 a.m. It was Thursday, December 8, 1988, and the jack-up oil rig *Rowan Gorilla 1* was finally underway, being towed by the powerful Dutch salvage tug, *Smit London*. It was a gorgeous, sunny morning. The air was crisp and everyone was relaxed as they started the long journey from Halifax, Nova Scotia, to the North Sea by way of the Azores. As the rig passed Chebucto Head on its way out of Halifax Harbour, a pod of 30 or so dolphins frolicked, playfully flinging themselves off the rig's bow wave as the tug and rig made their way into the Atlantic Ocean. Many of the crew clustered on the bow to watch. Among them was Clinton Cariou, the rig's senior barge engineer. As he watched the racing dolphins, Clinton

The *Smit London*

heard someone comment that they were a good omen. He had no reason to disagree with that sentiment.

Clinton had been working for the Rowan Company for six and a half years. He joined the *Rowan Gorilla 1* in Belle Chasse, Louisiana, in November 1983 and was aboard for the maiden voyage to the Sable Island area the next month. As senior barge engineer, he had many responsibilities, but chief among these were the safety, stability, and watertight integrity of the rig both while jacked up and afloat. For a rig that weighed in excess of 20,000 tons, stability was of paramount concern.

Viewed from above, the *Rowan Gorilla 1* was shaped like a large isosceles triangle, with the stern being the shorter base of the triangle and the other two longer sides joining at the bow. At each of the three corners were the long legs of the rig. They were constructed in a box frame manner, like one would see in a scaffold. When the rig was sitting idle in a harbour (stacked), or when it was being towed, the legs were largely out of the water, towering up to 150 metres in the air, approximately as tall as a 50-storey building. When the rig was engaged in a drilling operation, the legs were lowered until they hit the sea floor, and the platform was jacked up 30 centimetres above the water. Then the crew would pump 16,000 tons of sea water into the 18 "pre-load" tanks, which lined the outer perimeter in the hull of the rig. The dual purpose of this pre-loading was to drive the legs into the sea floor and to simulate storm type stresses on the rig to ensure its safety. The water was then pumped out and the rig was jacked up to its working height, leaving an "air gap" of 21 metres between the surface of the ocean and the bottom of the platform. The pre-load test was done with an air gap of only 30 centimetres because, if something went wrong, 30 centimetres wouldn't be far to fall. At a rig's working height of 21 metres, if a leg or the sea bottom gave out, it would be catastrophic and would kill everyone aboard. It was one of Clinton's jobs to supervise this test.

Personal experience played a role in Clinton's aware-ness of the importance of stability to the rig. On the maiden voyage of the *Rowan Gorilla 1* in December 1983, a grim situation had developed when the rig's tow wire had parted in a storm as it had taken a beating from 50-knot winds in five-metre seas. It had been a harsh education with a sharp learning curve for the young barge engineer trainee. Adrift with its stern to the pounding waves, the rig had developed numerous cracks in its stern pre-load tanks. Down-flooding had caused the stern to sink so low the seas had begun boarding. Green water had flooded the aft decks, pushing the stern down farther with every wave as the ocean had tried to drown the rig. The violent motion had also caused the legs, which had been raised, to oscillate, creating huge stresses on their supports. These stresses in turn had created cracks in the hull beneath the supports. With each swing of the legs, the cracks had gaped, allowing more water to flood in. Then the cracks had closed as the legs swung back the other way. The crew had managed to control the damage and the pumps had kept up with the inflow of water. On Christmas Day, they had managed to reconnect the towline, and the rig had limped into St. Margaret's Bay outside Halifax without further incident.

The *Rowan Gorilla 1* had stayed in St. Margaret's Bay for repairs. One of the repairs made was to weld extra gussets, or supports, in all the pre-load tanks. This upgrade was meant to strengthen the tanks in case the rig encountered that situation again. The rig was then towed out to the Sable Island area to drill in a number of locations for the next five years.

A view from the *Smit London,* two hours
before the *Rowan Gorilla 1* was abandoned

There was a bond that developed among the men
aboard. "We were all young," recalled Clinton. "I was only 27.
We worked hard and we played hard. We had two weeks off
and we'd all get together and come downtown to Halifax."
They worked 12-hour shifts for two weeks and then had
two weeks of leisure time ashore the entire time they were
employed on the rig.

Eventually the contract expired, and with no potential work, the *Rowan Gorilla 1* was towed to Halifax Harbour, where it sat idle for months. Facing a monthly cost of approximately $30,000 to keep a rig "stacked" in port, the owners shopped the *Rowan Gorilla 1* for work outside Eastern Canadian waters. By mid-November they had lined up a contract in the oil- and gas-rich North Sea. The rig was prepared for the long trans-Atlantic ocean tow.

It was the luck of the draw that Clinton would be the senior barge engineer for the trip, which would begin at the start of his two-week rotation. In the two weeks prior to the voyage, his counterpart prepared the rig for the tow. Shipping containers full of equipment were welded to the deck to keep them from shifting during the crossing. Calculations were made for which ballast tanks to flood so the rig would ride the ocean swells in a stable and smooth manner. The rig's derrick and cantilever were skidded to a more secure position and locked into place. These tasks and many others were necessary before the rig could sail. During his last week off, Clinton went aboard to confer and coordinate with the relief senior barge engineer. Clinton felt confident in the preparations that had been made. As he said, "There were concerns, but you have concerns with any tow. With the ocean tow, it's always a different beast."

A 36-hour window of good weather was forecast to start on December 8, giving them enough time to get a jump ahead of any storms that would track up the eastern seaboard.

Alexander Rijnsaardt (pronounced Reyn-hard) was the master of the *Smit London*. With 26 years of sea-going experience, he had been a Master Mariner for 15 years, all with Smit International. While he had never before towed an oil rig as a tug's captain, he had experience with trans-Atlantic towings of oil rigs as a mate on a tug. He had a lot of experience in crossing the Atlantic Ocean, and he had never experienced a towline failure the entire time he had been a captain.

Captain Rijnsaardt sent Jan Brinkman to the *Rowan Gorilla 1* as a tow rider. Jan would be a liaison between Rig Superintendent Jeff Cox and Captain Rijnsaardt. If the towline parted, Jan would be responsible for supervising the reconnection on the rig. Finally, they were ready to sail.

**Storms and Stress**
The inherent unreliability of weather forecasting was a problem to be considered. Captain Rijnsaart was planning to take a more southerly course toward the Azores before turning north for the British Isles to avoid the worst of the weather. One advantage of this route was that it would enable them to avoid the possibility of freezing spray, which is deadly to ships. The spray off an extremely cold ocean can freeze on a ship instantly, adding layers of ice that severely affect the ship's stability. One cubic metre of ice weighs one ton, and it doesn't take long for enough ice to build up to make a ship so top-heavy that it capsizes.

The trip was routine until Monday, December 12. The

weather had been cooperative, with moderate winds and swells. When they were 800 kilometres southeast of Halifax, Captain Rijnsaardt set an easterly course for a more direct route across the Atlantic. By early morning, however, the weather turned on them, and the winds and seas began to build. The storm was unexpected, and problems arose immediately. The seas were six metres, and the motion was creating difficulties aboard the *Smit London.*

Captain Rijnsaardt checked the forecasts and saw there was a cyclonic storm to their west. Yet another developing storm was approaching from the southwest. Things were not looking good. The winds were going to pick up to 50 to 65 knots, and the seas would build to 10 metres. He shifted the tug's course to the southeast in an attempt to steer the rig away from the volatile weather heading their way.

Aboard the rig, the crew jacked the legs down eight metres to storm position to dampen the rig's motion. They began routine inspections of the pre-load tanks and compartments to ensure their watertight integrity. The tanks had sounding tubes — five-centimetre vertical pipes from the tank bottom to the deck of the rig — so one only had to pop the cap and drop in a plumb bob to check for water. Clinton hoped the new gussets welded in the tanks would maintain their integrity and remain dry.

Things went well through the night and the next morning, but at around noon on the 13th, they discovered that the steady pounding from severe seas had opened several small cracks in the guides that supported the port and starboard legs. The situation was declining on the *Smit London,* as well.

The towing bar across the tug's stern was covered by a plastic composite protector to keep the braided steel towline from chaffing under the intense friction generated by towing the massive oil rig. As the towline protectors wore out, they would be replaced. With the rig's legs in the storm position, there was greater drag on the *Smit London,* which made for greater wear on the towline. Throughout the morning the towline had worn through the protectors quickly, and there was a limited supply of protectors. Captain Rijnsaardt kept Jeff Cox abreast of these developments, and at 4 p.m. they decided to raise the legs of the rig to their normal transit position, three and a half metres below the hull. Immediately, the *Rowan Gorilla 1* began bucking harder in the waves. By 8 p.m. they had to drop the legs again to the storm position, which brought more danger to the tug.

Now in nine-metre seas, the tug was making no progress and was in severe danger of being dragged under by the oil rig. As Clinton recounts, "We'd be on a crest and the *Smit London* would be in a trough and the tug is trying to maintain control so it doesn't get buried by a wave. What happens is the tug comes down the other side of the wave, the line comes tight and the weight of the rig just buries it."

Captain Rijnsaardt decided the only solution was to turn and run with the seas until the storm passed. They fought their way through the night until daylight on the morning of December 14, but by then the rig was beginning to take on water in other compartments, including one of the pre-load tanks.

Rig superintendent Jeff Cox was extremely concerned to learn that they were taking on water, especially given the forecasts for worsening weather. He spent most of his time in the control room taking reports, conferring with his staff, and deciding on courses of action to keep them afloat. That morning, in a phone call to company headquarters in Houston, the engineers decided the only way to deal with the fractures in the tanks was by entering them and welding doubler plates to repair them. This decision meant that Clinton would be headed into the damaged pre-load tank, number 14, with Wayne Decoste, the rig's welder. They wouldn't be going alone. Randy Pippy and Dale Smith would be going with them to check the shale shaker house, which was beside pre-load tank 14. During drilling operations, the mud from the well is pumped into the shale shaker house to filter out the crumbled rock created by the drilling. The rock is analysed by the geologists aboard to determine the quality of gas in the well.

It was getting very dangerous going out on deck. With every wave that slammed into the rig, green water would wash across the afterdecks, but there was no thought of refusing to face the danger. They were fighting for their lives and had to cope quickly with every problem that arose, no matter what the risk. As the four men made their way to the shale shaker house, a monstrous wave broke over the stern. Three of them managed to race up a set of stairs ahead of the wave, but Randy Pippy was caught below. Tons of water slammed into him, tossing him about like a tissue in the wind. Terror struck and he groped blindly to find something, anything, to keep from being washed overboard. The fingers of one hand caught a grate, and he strained to hang on dearly until the wave receded, dropping him to the deck. He sputtered and struggled to catch his breath before getting to his feet. The other men helped him clamber up the ladder, all of them awestruck and grateful that he'd survived.

Once they arrived at tank 14, Clinton and Wayne went inside with a VHF radio and a flashlight to make their measurements. The other two men closed the hatch and sealed it before carrying on to the shale shaker house. When Clinton and Wayne were finished, they'd have to use their radio to call Randy and Dale to open the hatch and release them from their watery prison.

Engulfed in the dark, cold, dankness of the tank, Clinton and Wayne discovered a horizontal hairline fracture, 38 centimetres long. With every smash of a wave on the stern, the crack appeared almost to breathe, expanding to a five-centimetre gap that allowed water to shoot three metres into the compartment. The pair shivered in the cold and wet, struggling to take their measurements by the light of their flashlight. It was slow going because they were interrupted by the bursts of water that would come shooting into the tank. It would be almost impossible to bring a tank of acetylene in and try to weld the fracture. It was hard enough just trying to take measurements. However, if it would help save the rig, then that's exactly what they would do. After 15 minutes, they radioed Randy and Dale, who opened the hatch to release them from the eerie darkness. Timing the waves, they scrambled to cross the decks and made it back inside to relative safety.

While the situation was tense, Clinton didn't yet feel it was critical, and he was too busy to be truly afraid. He had experience in this type of weather, and he had been in 10-metre seas before. While he was very concerned, he wasn't unduly alarmed because they were managing to keep up with the ingress of water. However, by that afternoon the waves had mounted to 12 metres, and it didn't appear as though they had finished building. The crew could no longer go outside on the main decks, which were constantly awash.

The situation worsened when the containers welded to the deck were ripped free by the constant stress of the pounding seas. Five massive shipping containers, each 12 x 6 x 2.5 metres and loaded with equipment, broke free in succession. They skidded back and forth on the deck, wreaking havoc as they ripped through hull fittings for the electrical connections, opening more gaping holes for water to enter the rig. Clinton stood on the top deck with some of the other crew members, watching as the spectacle unfolded. "The one that caused the main problem was a container that had about 8,000 pounds of pump parts," he recalls. "It was welded to the deck and broke loose and slammed around for a good 20 minutes. It finally went through the handrail, and where it went through, the handrail looked like it had been cut. It probably travelled a good 40 feet across the deck then cut the handrail completely off. It didn't bend it, it took it out cleanly. It was destroying everything. Breaking off through hull connections for electrical, it would hit the guard around them and shear them off cleanly. Water would be dripping through the hull and decks onto the machinery deck." Now water was pouring into the hull from above as well as below. It was everywhere, and the crew faced a daunting battle to keep themselves afloat.

The *Smit London* was coping with problems of its own, and it would be a very long and hard night for the crews of both vessels. The towline was whipping back and forth across the tow bar on the stern of the tug as it crawled up one 12-metre wave and down another. While the danger of being pulled under had eased, the tug's crew still encountered great difficulty in controlling its tow. By 11 p.m., the towline had worn through the last of the protectors, and the following seas were creating huge stresses on the line. The waves had built to 15 metres, and as the tug rose and fell, the line would snap taut and then release. With the last protector gone and the tow wire tension metre pegging out at 280 tons, before fluttering back to zero, the towline was wearing quickly. The probability that the line would break had increased dramatically. Once that happened, there would be no way to reconnect the line in that storm, leaving the rig to spin and drift out of control.

On the rig it was water, water, everywhere. It was pouring through cracks in the pre-load tanks, coming in through loose hatches, and pouring down through the holes for electrical connections. The crew was frantically scrambling to pump it out so they could stay afloat and survive the night. They formed roving parties that would move around the rig to look for new damage. One of these groups reported to Jeff that the main hatch to the mud room was gone. Jeff had no idea if it had been torn loose by containers or by suction from boarding seas breaking over the deck. Not that it mattered. It meant more downflooding and yet another problem that had to be addressed quickly. Now the rig was in the unorthodox situation of having water in compartments that had no pumps. The crew had to brainstorm new solutions.

It was around 2 a.m. on the morning of the 15th when the towline finally wore through and snapped. Clinton was actually surprised it hadn't given way earlier. Jeff tried manoeuvring with the rig's thrusters for a while, but it seemed the thrusters didn't make much difference, and when water started collecting in the port thruster room, he had to shut them down.

The rig was now being pummelled by the worst the storm had to offer. The winds were constantly 60 knots or more, and the seas were almost 20 metres. The waves were so high that they were washing over the cantilever and striking the derrick, which was 10 metres above the deck in the centre of the rig.

There was still no talk of abandoning the rig. During a storm, there is a psychological barrier in leaving a huge vessel to take your chances in a little lifeboat. If these huge waves were washing over this massive oil rig and creating this kind of havoc, what would they do with a lifeboat? Besides, the crew were still keeping up with the flooding. While the rig's stern was almost constantly under water, their improvised repairs seemed to be doing the trick. They were holding their own.

Clinton knew they were in serious trouble. At one point, a crewman wanted Clinton to go outside to see something on the top deck, 15 metres above the waterline. "I walked about eight metres from the radio room and couldn't see ahead 'cause there was no light, no depth perception, but I turned around and looked back. We were in the trough of a wave and I could actually see the top of the wave looming over the radio room. I told him, 'You know, I didn't really need to see that.'"

To complicate matters, in some compartments the crew couldn't hear each other. "It was extremely noisy on the machinery deck from the rig banging and flexing in the seas and wind," says Clinton. "Because of the way the cantilever was designed it was bending as well, so you had a double

A 35-foot wave breaking over the rig of the *Rowan Gorilla 1*

dose. You could see some of the metal on the machinery deck flexing. We were terrified. We couldn't communicate. If you wanted to talk to someone five feet away, you had to cup your hands around your mouth and yell." As Clinton was standing on the machinery deck, he noticed a fire bell on the wall had been activated. He couldn't hear it over the agonized screaming of the steel in the rig; rather, he could *see* the clapper banging on the bell. The din of the rig continued through most of the night.

In the air compressor room, the pumps had lost

suction. The screens over the pump intakes in their deep sumps were clogged up with soaked and soggy cardboard. The crew cleaned them up, only to have them fill later with loose bolts, which were impossible to clear. They opened the enormous watertight doors on the air compressor room to allow the water, which was two metres deep, to flow into the next room, where the sumps were clear. The crew built sluices and dams out of wooden pallets, plywood, or whatever else was handy to redirect the water to the nearest functioning sumps.

Some problems were especially difficult to deal with in a night filled with difficult problems. There was a metal skirt, 30 centimetres tall, surrounding the electrical motor control centre, yet water was slopping over it, endangering the power supply. With no way to pump the water out of this area, the crew built a tall, plywood dam to keep the water out. This task was not easy in the pitching, rolling rig. As Clinton recalls, "We're in 60-foot seas trying to hammer little finishing nails to make dams. You're doing what you have to do to survive."

Moving in these water-filled rooms was a problem in itself. A wave would strike the rig, making it surge forward, which would create waves inside that were large enough to knock people off their feet. It got so bad that crew members were holding on to gussets inside the rooms on the machinery deck so they could keep on their feet. Equipment had broken loose and was strewn everywhere inside the rig. In the galley and infirmary, items had been knocked loose from shelves and cabinets and were strewn all over the floor. Despite the conditions, the crew was busy working hard. By the middle of the night they were scrambling to fix things, even though they were gripped by terror. The stewards made sandwiches and coffee for the crew and passed them around, despite the shambles in the galley.

Jeff was in the control room being peppered with information about new situations with which he had to deal. The rig was drowning and the pumps weren't keeping up. Bill Charchuck and George Campbell had a suggestion that they courageously volunteered to carry out. They thought the most effective way to eliminate the largest amount of water was to reconfigure the shale shaker house pumps so they would pump water instead of mud. They could also open some valves that would allow them to pump water from lower in the rig as well as getting rid of the water in the mud pits and the shaker house.

By now, nobody was allowed out because ponderous waves were sweeping unchecked across the deck, but the situation was so critical that Bill and George felt compelled to brave the elements in an effort to save the rig. They had to time it right in order to pull it off. With the thrusters gone and no control over the rig's drift, the *Rowan Gorilla 1* was slowly rotating in circles. They waited until the end of the rig opposite their path was taking the brunt of the beating from the storm and then took off for the shale shaker house. The wind shrieked at them as they slipped and stumbled across the slick decks. They charged inside the shale shaker house and slammed the hatch shut behind them. Working quickly, they managed to reconfigure the pumps and open the necessary valves. Success! But now the rig was facing in the wrong direction and the ocean was ripping across the decks. It would tear them from the rig if they attempted to leave their shelter.

Bill and George waited impatiently for another 20 to 30 minutes, until the rig had been spun by the storm so their path was once again to the lee of the wind and the fury of the waves. Then they scampered across the darkened decks to where everyone anxiously awaited their return.

By morning, things actually seemed to be looking up. Although the rig was still in 18-metre seas, the wind had subsided considerably. Miraculously, the crew members were still holding their own and managing to keep up with the flooding. Daylight had a huge impact on their state of mind. They could finally see without artificial lighting. The worst the rig had listed was six degrees at the stern, and that hadn't changed through the night. Then the final nail in the coffin of the *Rowan Gorilla 1* was hammered home.

At around 7 a.m., the power failed. The crew realized it was a complete and utter blackout when the emergency generators didn't engage. Getting the power back on became the most urgent priority. They had to get electricity going to the pumps again. The relative optimism they had started to feel with the arrival of daylight quickly left when they were back to using flashlights inside. A team was sent to repair the generator, but by the time they had located the problem and fixed it, they had lost nearly 30 minutes of pumping time. By 8 a.m. the rig had lost another degree in the stern.

Clinton believes they might have saved the rig if the power hadn't gone out. "About an hour later, we'd almost arrived at the point of no return. We had all the power back up and the pumps functioning. We'd lost a degree in the stern, and then another degree, so we went from seven to eight to nine degrees and we couldn't recover."

By noon, the situation on the rig was becoming desperate. The list had increased to 12 degrees and the down-flooding was out of control. Throughout the night, Jeff had been in close contact with Captain Rijnsaardt. The veteran tug captain had retired to his stateroom to read a report he had on the sinking of the *Dan Prince*, a similar rig to the *Rowan Gorilla 1*. In 1980, the *Dan Prince* had encountered a storm, its towline had parted, and it had taken on water and was wallowing in heavy seas with its stern awash before it capsized and sank. The parallels were striking. Captain Rijnsaardt radioed the rig and told Jeff what he had discovered in the report. Clinton and tourpushers Glenn White and Bill Charchuck had discussions with Jeff on the same matter. They had lost too much stability, and Clinton didn't think the rig could recover.

It was Jeff's call. He was responsible for the $80 million oil rig and was reluctant to abandon it. A significant number of ship captains never declare a Mayday, even as their ship is sinking underneath them. Jeff was an exceptionally balanced and capable manager, despite his youth and lack of experience in the offshore. He consulted with his crew rather than dictating orders. Clinton puts it this way: "I think the reason he listened is he's a pretty smart guy and had a good handle on his people. When there was a problem he didn't understand, he was more than willing to look to those with experience around him and take their advice, which takes a pretty big man to do that."

Throughout the last few days, Jeff had been concerned about the possibility of abandoning the rig. He knew that the forecasts called for the weather to abate in the next day, and he was hoping the rig could hold on until then. At one point, he was in the control room with Glenn White. The sun had miraculously broken through, and, looking behind them, Jeff could see a colossal wave, larger than any they'd encountered, roaring up on them. Just as they were in the trough, Jeff turned to Glenn and said, "If we come back from this wave, we'll be okay."

The wave steamrolled over the rig. After it passed, there was another huge wave, and then another. They kept coming, each one larger than the last. Jeff and Glenn were well above the waterline, but they were still looking *up* at these waves as they rolled over the rig. Given the way the situation had degenerated, Jeff knew the crew had to abandon. They would take their chances in the monstrous seas in their little life capsule.

## Little Lifeboat in Large Seas

There was still much to be done. Once the decision to abandon was made, everyone gathered on the top deck to review procedures and make preparations. The excellent training they'd received from Survival Systems in Halifax had gone a long way to ensuring things were efficient and everyone felt confident. Still, a few minor problems arose. Clinton's search for seasick pills and patches for the crew was more difficult than he'd anticipated. The infirmary was a disaster area, with cabinets knocked over and their contents strewn all over the floor. Eventually, he found the medication and made his way topside to distribute it to the crew prior to abandoning. Everyone had warm clothing on under their survival suits, and before they boarded the lifeboat, a head count was made. Although everyone was nervous about taking to the sea in the tiny lifeboat, they were ready to go.

Clinton was trained in small-craft handling and would be the coxswain for the boat. He still didn't feel great about leaving the rig. It's one thing to buzz around the pedestrian safety of Halifax Harbour, quite another to be taking to the tiny craft in 16-metre seas.

As he made he way to the radio room, Jeff Cox also felt apprehension about leaving the safety of the big rig and facing the sea in the little life capsule. Up to that point the *Smit London* had relayed most of the information between the rig and Halifax Coast Guard Radio, but there was one last transmission that Jeff had to do on his own. Picking up the microphone, he selected 2182 and made a quick but deliberate Mayday call, giving the rig's name and position and the fact they were abandoning. With no time to wait for replies, he made his way directly to the lifeboat station.

Discussing the launch with the mechanic and the electrician, the senior crew went over all the potential hazards and scenarios. Among their concerns were loading the boat, launching without hitting the rig, and ensuring the smooth release of the boat hooks. Once they had everything worked out, they loaded the boat and were ready to go. They would be dropping down from 12 metres above the water, and the waves were still a substantial 16 metres tall.

On the *Rowan Gorilla 1*'s lifeboats, the brake release mechanism was outside the boat, so the hatch had to be open prior to launching. With the help of barge engineer trainee John Urbanczyk, Clinton had found a way to overcome the problem. John stood at the closed hatch ready to release the brake handle when Clinton gave the word. Sitting in the coxswain's seat and looking out the windows, Clinton waited until a wave hit them. Then, after it subsided and he could see, he hollered, "Go," and John opened the hatch, pulled the handle, and then slammed and sealed the hatch again. They dropped the 12 metres steadily and smoothly until they were just above the surface of the ocean. Clinton pulled the ring that unlocked the boat hooks. All that was needed now was a wave to lift the boat slightly, displacing its weight so the hooks would drop free and they'd be free and clear of the rig.

John had the ratchet for the emergency release mechanism in case anything went wrong.

The first wave hit them, but only the crest caught them, and instead of lifting the boat enough to release the hooks, it banged them against the rig. "Get the ratchet," hollered Clinton. Just as John grabbed it, another wave picked them up, the boat hooks dropped, and they were free and clear.

Gunning the throttle, Clinton immediately turned hard to port to get away from the dying rig. They hit their first real wave and had a few anxious moments. The potential for the wave to lift them up and drop them right back on the rig or slam them into it was very real. Jeff was on the radio with the *Smit London*, which gave them a course of 90 degrees to sail directly away from the massive structure. Aboard the *Smit London*, Captain Rijnsaardt had posted one team of lookouts to keep an eye on nothing but the lifeboat and another to keep a watch on the *Rowan Gorilla 1*. He knew that the *Rowan Gorilla 1* was drifting at seven knots, whereas the lifeboat could make only six knots, so it had to head on a perpendicular course to keep from being run over by the huge oil rig.

Seasickness swept through the lifeboat. The patches the crew had placed behind their ears were said to be very effective in combating seasickness, but they hadn't worn them long enough for the medication to take effect. "I'd say that from the time we hit the water, within 90 seconds ... there were 23 people sick out of the 27 aboard." Clinton said.

"Once the first person throws up, it just sweeps right through the boat."

Clinton didn't suffer a bout of seasickness himself, probably because he was busy driving the boat and could see the waves as they were coming. While the smell was a factor initially, shortly thereafter they all suffered from olfactory fatigue. The human body has an amazing ability to adapt, and pretty soon no one aboard could smell the stench anymore, despite buckets of vomit on the floor and everywhere else.

Once they were roughly 100 metres from the rig, Clinton announced they were clear and everyone cheered and applauded despite the nausea. It seemed as though the worst of the danger was over, but Clinton was having a difficult time with the heading they were given by the *Smit London*. Shortly after he had made his announcement, they were hit by a massive wave that broke over them and buried the little lifeboat. "The wave broke right over top of us," remembers Clinton. "I saw it at the last minute and tried to turn, too late. It buried the boat completely. We were under water and it was black."

Aboard the *Smit London* the lookouts didn't know if the lifeboat would recover. The wave had hit the lifeboat with such force that Wayne Decoste banged his head on the hull. When he rubbed his head it was wet, and he thought the hull had been breached. "Aw geez boys, she's breaking up," he said. Alarmed, Jeff made his way over to check it out. Feeling the side of the capsule, he realized that it was indeed wet, but it was condensation from their breath that made it so rather than the hull being holed. Everyone gave a sigh of relief.

Clinton radioed the *Smit London* and told them he was going to change course. He was somewhat blind running straight up the waves, and he needed to see the wave top in order to gauge if it would break. If it did, he could turn to port and give the engine hard throttle to beat the break, or chop back the power hard so the wave would break in front, rather than crash down on top of them. Driving the little boat hard and for all it was worth, he was pleasantly surprised by its relatively nimble response.

Once they had cleared the rig, Clinton knew they had made the right decision about abandoning. The concern about being in the small lifeboat, which had worried him prior to the launch, dissolved when he discovered that this little boat was handling extremely well. Looking back at the doomed oil rig, he could see the portion that was supposed to be high and dry was completely submerged.

They sailed on for another 45 minutes and then the engine in the lifeboat quit. Clinton attempted to restart the engine. It turned over but wouldn't catch. He spun the helm hard over to port to see what would happen. For some reason, as long as the helm was hard over to port or starboard, they had a much easier time of things. Without the engine driving it ahead, the lifeboat just bobbed over the waves rather than being forced under.

As it turned out, having the engine quit was a blessing

in disguise for a number of reasons. One advantage was that the crew could communicate with one another without having to yell over the din of the engine. The temperature inside the lifeboat also became more tolerable. With their heavy clothing and survival suits, the crew was already too warm. Add to that a diesel engine running at 93 degrees Celcius and the heat quickly became excruciating. Because of the huge seas, they couldn't take a chance on opening a hatch — one wave could flood the capsule and sink them. So when the engine quit, the dissipation of some of the heat was welcomed. Unfortunately, even after the engine shut down, the heat caused another complication for the inhabitants of the lifeboat — dehydration.

The bins in which provisions were stored were clearly labelled and very accessible. The drinking water was under the middle row of seats and it was just a matter of popping the lid with a screwdriver to open the bin. The crew had been trained not to drink water for the first 24 hours after abandoning. There was a finite supply of water, and because one didn't know how long one would be adrift, conventional wisdom was to conserve supplies. However, most in the lifeboat had vomited and were sweating in the heat, and they quickly became dehydrated. It wasn't long before someone mentioned that they were thirsty and needed water. Remembering their training, they initially decided against breaking open the water provisions, but then their lips started to crack and their tongues became dry and swollen. Jeff decided that with

36 seats in the boat and only 27 filled, they would drink the water for the nine absentees. "This was a defining moment in respect to our morale," Clinton recalls.

Aside from feeling better both physically and emotionally, their thought processes became sharper. Losing 2 percent of the body's capacity for water means losing 25 percent of one's ability to think rationally. When the moment of rescue comes, making a mistake can mean the difference between life and death — clarity of thought becomes critical. Drinking the water had been the right decision. They were all starting to feel better. With no engine, Clinton stepped down from the coxswain's seat after an hour and someone else took over to keep a lookout and ensure the tiller was kept hard over.

It was around 4 p.m., two and a half hours after abandoning, when they got a call from Captain Rijnsaardt aboard the *Smit London*. The lookouts aboard the tug who were assigned to watch the rig reported that the once robust and proud *Rowan Gorilla 1* had capsized on its aft legs and had sunk.

Aboard the lifeboat, the news left Jeff feeling disheartened and somewhat melancholy. He'd hoped that the rig would weather the storm and that they would somehow be able to reboard it, make temporary repairs, and nurse it into port. Jeff proposed a minute of silence for the rig, which they had fought so hard to save and which had provided them all a good livelihood for the past five years.

After their moment of silence, Wayne Decoste, the

welder, said, "Man, am I ever glad that thing sank." When a bemused Jeff asked why Wayne was glad the rig was gone, Wayne explained that he'd rushed to get his gear when the word came to abandon, but when he tried to open his locker to get his passport and wallet, he realized he'd left his key in the change room. Spotting a fire axe next to the locker, he realized he could use the axe to knock the lock off. He lined it up and swung from the heels, but the deck heaved just as he was about to make contact and he destroyed the two lockers next to his own, which was untouched. After that miscalculation, he figured he'd better just abandon his passport and wallet along with the rig and made his way to the boat deck. "I didn't know how to tell you that, but I'm telling you now," he confessed. Wayne was well liked and known for his jokes and stories. This confession broke the tension and brought about some sorely needed laughter.

By now, the crew was feeling much better. The boat was riding well, they had warded off dehydration, and they were alive. Given the stress they had undergone on the rig, they now knew they were in a much more secure position in the lifeboat. Creating more of a concern for those aboard was how their families were taking the news. Aboard the lifeboat, they *knew* they were safe and sound; their families had no idea what kind of condition they were in. Their loved ones would be nerve-wracked until the men were plucked from the lifeboat and returned safely home. Clinton could speak to this from personal experience. "When the *Ocean Ranger* went down, my father was on the Sedco 706. So when that happened, I was greatly afraid for my father who was out in the storm at the time." It was hard for the crew knowing that their families were in the dark about their situation.

The Rescue Coordination Centre (RCC) in Halifax had been following the situation closely through Halifax Coast Guard Radio. Both the *Smit London* and Jeff aboard the *Rowan Gorilla 1* had been speaking to them since the rig had suffered structural damage in the first storm. Halifax Coast Guard Radio kept checking in with them every four hours after the towline had parted. A Mayday was finally declared when Jeff called RCC to tell them he was abandoning the rig. Dispatching the Canadian Coast Guard ship *Sir William Alexander* and Canadian navy ship HMCS *Ottawa* from Halifax, RCC also diverted the Canadian Department of Fisheries vessel *Leonard J. Cowley* toward the distress scene. The ships were too far away to make any immediate difference, with the exception of the HMCS *Ottawa*. If it could get within a few hundred kilometres, it could pick the survivors out of the life capsule using its Sea King helicopter. RCC also dispatched an Aurora — a four-engine, long-range search-and-rescue aircraft — to fly over the capsule and follow it until a rescue could be attempted. At around 5:30 p.m., the Aurora arrived and began to circle the lifeboat, but until the weather improved, all the survivors could do was drift in the heavy seas and wait.

Aboard the lifeboat, the crew was coping. Being seated

in one spot for so long was causing cramps, so each person took a turn standing up to stretch while everyone else supported him so he wouldn't fall as the lifeboat crawled up or down a wave. They swapped seats to keep their blood circulating and took the arms out of their survival suits to dissipate the heat. They did what they could to avoid physical discomfort. They talked, told stories and jokes, and sang songs to keep from being bored. As is often the case when people are stuck in a stressful situation with nothing to do but talk, they sometimes touched on deeper personal issues. Clinton had proposed to his fiancée four days before departing Halifax, but he hadn't told anyone. He did so in the lifeboat. Most of the crew had been up for more than 36 hours straight, and those who were able to, took advantage of the opportunity to sleep.

Throughout the night the Aurora continued to circle the lifeboat, making low passes and dropping flares, which had a marvellous effect on the crew's morale. The crew members were in constant communication with the Aurora, which would call to say it was making another flare drop. The light from the powerful flares would pour into the lifeboat through the windows around the coxswain's seat.

The voice of the pilot in the night helped raise spirits, but it also drained the batteries on the radio. This eventuality had been anticipated, so the crew had given John Urbanczyk one battery to hold on to for the rescue attempt in case the rest had died. He was told to put it in his pocket and not give it to them, no matter how they pleaded or threatened. Sure enough, the next morning they were down to their last battery in the radio, which was fading quickly, but no matter what they said to John he maintained his fortitude and held on to it until he was certain they were about to be rescued, be it by helicopter or by ship.

The *Smit London* was nowhere to be seen throughout the night, but it was hovering not too far away. Captain Rijnsaardt had dropped back because he didn't want to inadvertently run over the little lifeboat. With the heaving seas, he couldn't maintain consistent contact with it visually, and he couldn't get a radar return on it at all. So he dropped back to a safe distance and trusted the Aurora to keep the lifeboat in sight.

By morning, the weather was much improved. The seas were down to four metres, although it was a confused, choppy sea, and the swells were not running in a predictable direction. Then the call came that although the HMCS *Ottawa* was within range for the helicopter rescue, the Sea King had broken down and wouldn't be able to make the trip immediately. Captain Rijnsaardt requested that he be allowed to go over to try to pick the survivors up in a Zodiac, but RCC felt it would be too dangerous and advised against it. So they were back to waiting once again.

Aboard the lifeboat, the chief steward of the rig was a diabetic and was starting to feel ill. Jeff radioed this information over to the *Smit London*. Checking the weather and seeing that it was going to get worse, Captain Rijnsaardt decided that the diabetic crewman needed some food right away, and that the handheld VHF radio on the lifeboat would need fresh batteries. Calling the lifeboat, he told Jeff about the Zodiac, gave him his advice, and let Jeff make the call. Jeff consulted the crew, and they decided that they would try it, and if there were no problems, perhaps they could even attempt a transfer.

Captain Rijnsaardt sent three crewmen from the *Smit London* over to the lifeboat in the tug's three-metre Zodiac. When Jeff opened the hatch, the sight that met his eyes didn't inspire confidence. One crewman was pumping a hand bulb to keep the engine primed with gas, another crewman was bailing the Zodiac with a small pail, and the third crewman was working a foot pump to keep the Zodiac inflated. Jeff closed the door. He decided to let the crew of the raft sort out their situation, then maybe they could start the transfer.

"So they called back on the radio and said things were fixed up ... the problems were due to the weather and the fact the engine was cold. Once they got it warmed up it worked better. Those guys did one heck of a job," said Jeff.

Jeff felt that they could take back a couple of volunteers. Because Clinton had slept all night and hadn't been seasick, he volunteered to go with Glenn McDonald to take care of the ill steward on the trip to the *Smit London*. "We got to the *Smit London* and they had a Jacob's ladder ready," Clinton explains. "We had to climb maybe 15 or 20 feet after we timed the swell. We clambered up and then over the handrail in our

Gumby suits where a couple of crewmen received us."

Before going inside to be checked out and tended to, Clinton called Jeff and said the transfer went well. From that point, the Zodiac made a number of trips to ferry people back two and three at a time. If it had been any other lifeboat, Clinton thinks they wouldn't have been able to make a transfer. The handrails and bumper allowed an individual to stand securely on the outside in order to board the Zodiac.

Once everyone was safely aboard, the *Smit London* sailed back to Halifax. The lifeboat was left to bob until it sank. It was never recovered. When the crew arrived back in Halifax, the company rented an entire floor at one of the city's finest hotels for the week so that the survivors could rest up after their harrowing experience. Clinton only stayed a single night. With a new lease on life, he just wanted to go home to rest with his family and fiancée.

After any major marine incident, there are investigations and reports that analyse the sequence of events, as well as the causes and effects; then the agencies responsible make recommendations to enhance shipping safety. As a result of what occurred in the *Rowan Gorilla 1*'s life capsule, the instructions printed on the packaging for water in lifeboats has changed all over the world. They now state that you shouldn't drink for 24 hours *unless* dehydration is a factor, in which case water should be drunk immediately to alleviate the effects.

# Chapter 3
# The Sinking
## of the *Flare*

nn-Margret White was pacing from the chair in front of her console to the chart table and back again. It was just after 4:30 a.m. on January 16, 1998. With little more than a couple of hours to go until she was relieved on her first of two solitary night shifts as a radio operator at the Stephenville Coast Guard Radio in Newfoundland, it seemed the most efficient way to stay alert and beat the boredom and fatigue.

At 4:32 a.m., she'd just made her turn at the chart table when a call sliced through the room. It began with a few garbled words, but there was no mistaking the jittery voice hollering, "Mayday! Mayday! Mayday!"

Ann-Margret clearly remembers seeing the green light snap on, indicating which of the five peripheral antenna sites was receiving the call. It was being received at the Ramea Island site, which was 100 kilometres away. Rushing to her seat, she slapped on her headset and was answering the vessel within seconds, dearly hoping that other stations were hearing this call as well.

"What station calling? This is Stephenville Coast Guard Radio on channel 16. Say again, over?" she asked.

The response was a broken transmission of which a barely intelligible latitude, 4637 north, and perhaps a portion of a longitude, could be discerned as the signal cut in and out. In the background, frantic activity could be heard behind the panicky, unknown voice making the call, but there was no time to ponder this. If the ship was in trouble, it was critical to know its position to send assistance as quickly as possible. There was no firm longitude from the broken and distorted call she had just heard, so Ann-Margret took a stab at a reasonable longitude, hoping the voice would correct her. There was no response.

"Confirm 4637 north ..." she hesitated a split second, "... 5651 west, over?"

Dead air filled her headphones. Perhaps in his panic the sender was fumbling with the longitude, so she changed tack and asked a simpler question.

"How many persons on board, over?"

There was no response. Static filled her headset once again. The entire exchange took less than 30 seconds. She had to broadcast a Mayday relay, but she didn't have a proper position, never mind the name or description of the ship or any of the data that usually comprises a conventional call. Experience told her this call was no hoax, given the edgy, frightened panic in the voice she'd just heard. It was the real thing. Considering the overlapping radio coverage from several stations in the Cabot Strait area, Ann-Margret thought that perhaps someone else had heard the call more clearly than she and could supplement the scanty information she possessed. She called the Coast Guard radio stations in Sydney on Cape Breton Island, Nova Scotia, and in Placentia, Newfoundland, but to no avail. All they had heard was Ann-Margret's end of the exchange.

She made the relay with the little information she had. The chemical carrier *Stolt Aspiration* immediately replied that it was on the way and would be at the position in a couple of hours. Unfortunately, the radio operator had only heard Ann-Margret's end of the exchange, and there were no targets on the ship's radar. Calling the Marine Rescue Sub-Centre (MRSC) in St. John's, Newfoundland, Ann-Margret passed on the information she had as well as the course, speed, position, and estimated time of arrival for the *Stolt Aspiration* to be at the scene. Fairly certain of the latitude, she told the centre that the longitude was an estimate, and that the call was recorded on the dictaphone, which records everything on the air. Because it was locked away outside of the operations centre, she would have to call in the station manager before the call could be reviewed. The centre's personnel instructed her to call him in and continue the relays.

Calling the station manager, she apprised him of the situation and he said he would be right in. It was now 4:34 a.m. A scant two minutes had passed since Ann-Margret had received the Mayday.

As the MRSC informed the Rescue Coordination Centre in Halifax of events, Ann-Margret continued to broadcast Mayday relay calls. She later reflected that nothing in her experience had prepared her for the magnitude of what was happening.

Working as a radio operator often entails long stretches of tedious routine broken by short bursts of intense, heart-racing situations when mariners are in immediate danger. Ann-Margret had worked her share of these unusual cases over her seven years as a radio operator in Stephenville. She had worked all manner of marine incidents: sinking vessels, ships on fire, man overboards, and radio-medicals (when vessels would have injured or ill crewmen and would need a phone patch to a hospital and possibly require a medical evacuation). She had worked several incidents in which fatalities occurred, and these were made all the more difficult because they mostly involved fishing vessels carrying local people whom she sometimes knew. Fielding a phone call and answering questions from a wife whose husband was missing or a mother looking for a son in peril were some of the most troubling aspects of the job for her. "You think you brush it off, but you probably never do," she said. Fortunately, she wasn't alone in handling these situations. The RCC was always there to provide guidance and support.

Over at the RCC it had been a quiet night, and marine Search and Rescue (SAR) coordinator Steve Waller was hoping it would stay that way for the two hours or so left of his shift. His 12-hour shift had started the previous evening at 7 p.m. There were a couple of routine jobs, such as broken-down fishing vessels that needed a tow back to port, but by 9 p.m. everything had settled down.

It was quiet until exactly 4:37 a.m., when the call from MRSC Saint John's alerted Steve of the Mayday call heard by Stephenville. The maritime coordinator also informed Steve that the *Stolt Aspiration* was on its way to the distress position. By plotting the position on a chart and considering the call had been picked up by a radio station in Newfoundland, Steve realized that the MRSC would be the search coordinator and it would be MRSC's case to prosecute.

The RCC is a joint military/Coast Guard venture. Marine cases are handled by the Coast Guard maritime coordinator, whereas air cases are the responsibility of the military aeronautical coordinators at the main rescue centres across Canada. As aircraft involved in SAR cases are provided by the Canadian military, RCC is also responsible for assigning and tracking any aircraft to be used in a case. The primary base for rescue aircraft was Greenwood, Nova Scotia. The base provided Labrador helicopters and Hercules cargo planes configured for search and rescue. There were also Labrador helicopters at Gander, Labrador, and if necessary, they could get Sea King helicopters from the Shearwater airbase in Dartmouth, Nova Scotia. Therefore, the MRSC would coordinate the surface ships while RCC Halifax would control any aircraft involved in the search.

Twelve minutes later, as they were getting organized for the search, Steve answered the phone to hear RCC Norfolk, Virginia, on the line. An International Maritime Satellite (Inmarsat) distress alert had been received from a vessel called the *Flame.* Unfortunately, it was 70 kilometres south of the position that Steve had been given by Newfoundland. He now had to consider if this incident was the same incident or if it was a *different* ship in distress. At least now his office had the name of a ship that was in trouble — one critical piece of information they had been lacking until now. The ship had satellite communication, so it would be a larger, commercial ship, and they could now track down all kinds of information on it through Lloyd's Register of Shipping and other government agencies to which commercial, ocean-going vessels are required to report. Norfolk said they would fax the message right away, so Steve could read all the information it contained.

The Inmarsat system provides all communications for the world's commercial shipping through nine satellites parked in geo-stationary orbit approximately 35,600 kilometres above the equator. These satellites are stationed over the eastern Atlantic, the western Atlantic, the Pacific, and the Indian oceans and handle all modes of communication for ships: telephone, fax, telex, and even e-mail. Four of the satellites are operational; the other five are backups. Inmarsat also provides another highly critical function. There is a button on every ship's satellite terminal called the "panic" button. Once pressed, it sends a distress signal to the satellite on which the ship has logged in. From there, the distress message is bounced back down to an earth downlink station and through the network to an affiliated RCC, which may need to pass it on to the RCC closest to the area in which the distress has occurred. For this reason, Norfolk contacted RCC Halifax.

Besides Inmarsat, there are two other satellite systems that are crucial to the world's shipping. Any ship with a global positioning system (GPS) receiver can use the dozens of GPS satellites streaking around the globe in low-earth orbit to pinpoint its location within metres.

The third group of satellites are search-and-rescue satellites in low orbit called COSPAS-SARSAT. Every ocean-going ship has a device called an emergency position indicating radio beacon (EPIRB). With its antenna sticking out the top, an EPIRB looks like a soda cup with a straw, albeit slightly larger. It is attached to a ship with a bracket, but if the ship sinks, the EPIRB is designed to float free and immediately start broadcasting a signal to the SARSATs, providing information with which RCC can calculate the EPIRB's position and the name of the ship.

There was no EPIRB signal from the ship that was in trouble in Cabot Strait, which led Steve to believe that while the ship might be sinking, it hadn't sunk yet. However, the lack of communication was ominous. First, he had to establish if the Mayday call received by Stephenville and the Inmarsat distress alert were from the same ship, or if they were from two separate incidents. His gut instinct told him they were one and the same.

By 4:55 a.m. he had the Inmarsat distress message in hand and was looking it over. It contained a lot of information, the most important parts being the time of the alert, the ship's course, speed, and position, as well as when these details were last updated. Steve realized that the ship's GPS unit wasn't connected to the satellite terminal, which would have automatically kept the terminal updated with the ship's current position. Instead the ship's operator had to manually input the position. The message contained a time stamp that indicated a position update hadn't occurred for more than 12 hours. If the ship had been travelling at 12 or 13 knots, it could have travelled as far as 160 kilometres from the position indicated. He now felt more confident in the position relayed to him by the MRSC in St. John's.

There was another wrinkle in the information Steve had received. The name on the fax cover sheet from Norfolk had listed the vessel as the *Flare*. The name contained in the Inmarsat message was the *Flame*. "We had two different names on the same vessel and we had to confirm which one it was. I was fairly confident right from the beginning that it was some kind of typo. It was too close," Steve recalls.

However, the confusion over which name was correct needed to be resolved. Steve called the military operations centre and asked the staff to investigate both names. With two different yet very similar names and two positions that were so close, Steve was feeling more confident this distress call was actually the same incident, but he had to be absolutely certain.

The military operation centre called Steve back and told him that it was indeed the *Flare*. It had been renamed from the *Flame*, which accounted for the confusion. Steve was now sure of the name, but the position still had to be nailed down.

One of the options Steve had in confirming the position was contacting the agency responsible for enforcing the Eastern Canada traffic regulations for shipping: Ecareg Canada. All ships over 500 tons entering Canadian territorial waters were required to report to Ecareg 24 hours from Canadian waters with comprehensive information on their ship as well as providing data on their trip to Canada. Ecareg had a comprehensive database of all shipping bound for and departing from Canadian territorial waters. The most vital piece of information it had for Steve at this point was the ship's estimated time of arrival to the reporting line at Cabot Strait, the body of water between Newfoundland and Cape

Breton Island. Once Steve had that time, he worked back in calculating where the *Flare* would be based on its average speed. He realized it was highly probable it would have been at the Inmarsat position at the time of the Mayday call. He decided to call Ann-Margret in Stephenville to see how confident she was of the position she had taken.

Ann-Margret White had been extremely busy since she'd heard that first, broken call. St. Pierre radio had called looking for the position. Two ships had called to say they were on their way, so she took their information and passed it along to the MRSC in St. John's. St. John's also requested she call a ship named the *Flare* and told her that an Inmarsat distress message had been received from a ship with this name close to the position she'd given. She called at 5:21 a.m. and received no response from the vessel. She called again two minutes later. Still no response. Sydney Coast Guard Radio called to tell her the *Atlantic Freighter* — a ferry that makes regular runs between Sydney and Newfoundland — was diverting to the distress site and was eight hours away. She passed this news along to MRSC. Shortly thereafter, Steve called from RCC Halifax.

Only 17 minutes after Ann-Margret had called him, Stephenville station manager Derek White had driven the 12 kilometres from home, pulled the tape, and had listened to it. When Steve called, Derek had set it up so Steve could hear it as well. Steve was amazed that Ann-Margret could get any intelligible information from it, given the garbled transmission and the jittery panic in the voice on the other end. However, Ann-Margret possessed a well-developed ear from years of experience gleaning information from radio transmissions in all kinds of conditions, often from people who were difficult to understand. She told Steve that she was confident about the latitude, but the longitude was definitely suspect.

Despite the fact that Steve now felt confident in the Inmarsat position, RCC dispatched aircraft to check out both positions. Ann-Margret stayed on shift for another two hours coordinating communications. She didn't want to leave when her relief showed up, but midnight shifts take their toll, exhaustion was setting in, and she didn't want to leave any room for error. She did the smart thing and went home. Before she left, she was told not to come in for her second midnight shift; it would be covered. She refused this token of kindness, but it wasn't open to discussion. Ann-Margret's shift was ending, and Steve fully expected to be off in the next hour. He wanted to have as much done as possible when his relief arrived. For Steve Waller, the morning was anything but mundane.

Sifting through all the resources and assets at his disposal to assist in the search, Steve had to decide which ships would be useful and which would be too distant to be of assistance. Aside from Stephenville's Mayday relay, others were sent via a satellite broadcast within a discrete radius of the Mayday site. In all, 15 ships had responded to the

Mayday relays and of these 15, only four were told to stay on course for the search area; the rest were released to continue their journeys. The *Stolt Aspiration* was the only ship considered on scene within the initial search area closer to Newfoundland. The rest weren't expected to arrive until later in the day, so it would be up to the aircraft to do the bulk of the searching.

In addition to the four ships already on their way, MRSC St. John's dispatched two Coast Guard cutters, the *W. G. George* and the *W. Jackman*, out of Burin and Burgeo, Newfoundland, but neither would make it to the search area until later in the day. The Canadian frigate HMCS *Montreal* was also on the way but wouldn't get there until late afternoon. Fortunately for Steve, all the vessel movements were being coordinated by MRSC St. John's, which allowed him to work more closely with the air coordinators in Halifax.

Aircraft had been tasked almost immediately after the Mayday had come in. A Labrador search-and-rescue helicopter was the first to be tasked at 4:55 a.m. Given the designator Rescue 303, it was sent to the original distress position. Five minutes later, a four-engine, long-range Hercules cargo plane was tasked out of Greenwood and designated Rescue 306. It takes some time to prepare these aircraft to fly, but 25 minutes later, at 5:25 a.m., it was airborne and on its way. At 6:15 a.m., a Beech King Air, owned by Provincial Air Lines and leased by the Department of Fisheries for fishery patrol, was tasked as Rescue 01. Its pilot was instructed to get to a position just west of Cabot Strait and fly lines along latitude 4637 north. This request was based on Ann-Margret's confidence in the latitude she'd heard. King Air Rescue 01 would fly along that latitude and cross as many lines of longitude as possible in the hope of finding the stricken ship. By 6:25 a.m. it had arrived at the westernmost point and began flying its track. Two more helicopters would be dispatched later to help search the area.

In the freezing waters of Cabot Strait, time was of the essence. If the ship had sunk and people were in the water, they would die unless they were found and pulled out quickly. Even if they were wearing survival suits, it would only buy them an hour or two. A survival search would be done first. It was assumed that survivors would be actively cooperative in being found — setting off flares or looking for ways to signal anyone in the area of their presence. So the first sweep of the search area would be quick, and if nothing was found, the search would become more methodical.

Generally, when the position of a ship in trouble isn't known, a search of its last-known position is undertaken. Aircraft fly to the initial search point and run what is called an "expanding square search." Starting with a small square, they continue to move outward in ever-expanding squares, with the initial search position in the centre. For faster aircraft like the Hercules, their speed makes it impossible to cut the corners of a square as easily as a helicopter or a ship, so they're often assigned a "sector search." With the last known position as the central point, a circle is drawn around this area at an efficient radius. The aircraft fly across the circle, turn, and fly across it again, which cuts the circle into pie-shaped sectors. If the search area is extremely large, they may break it into boxes, with each aircraft assigned a box, and have them run a parallel track — crossing laterally across one end of the box, moving ahead a little, and doing it again until they've searched the entire boxed area.

With a lot of aircraft in the area, separation is critical so aircraft don't risk running into one another. The best way to maintain separation is to stagger altitudes. A helicopter may search an area at 150 metres while the Hercules may search the same area at 300 metres. All the aircraft are informed of all other aircraft in the area and how they fit in the overall picture. This coordination is usually done by the air controllers at RCC Halifax. If there are enough aircraft involved, however, or if the search area is extremely far offshore, in which case radio communication can become very difficult between RCC and the low-flying aircraft, an Aurora or Hercules will circle the site at an altitude of 3,000 metres and coordinate the aircraft involved. Communications are much easier to maintain with the high-flying Aurora.

Although the searchers now knew the ship was the *Flare*, and they had a description of the vessel, the search area was huge. Nobody knew what they would find — if anything — when they got there.

## Search and Rescue

The *Flare* was a bulk carrier of 16,400 gross tons that had been built in Japan 26 years earlier. With a black hull and a white superstructure aft, it had seven cargo holds forward of the superstructure, each separated by a watertight bulkhead. Six cranes on the deck were used to load cargo. The *Flare* had departed Rotterdam with a crew of 25 on December 30, bound for Montreal. The ship wasn't in the best of shape. Inspections had noted several defects, but they were within acceptable standards and not bad enough to keep it in port. A portable welding machine was placed aboard along with steel plating so a welder who was part of the crew could make some repairs on the voyage.

Almost immediately after the ship cleared the English Channel, the weather took a turn for the worse. The *Flare* carried no cargo and was lightly ballasted, which made for a rough ride. The crew was extremely concerned. The hull flexed noticeably and vibrated heavily when the ship ploughed through heavy seas, so much so that one crew member testified in the subsequent investigation that at times the deck cranes seemed to be touching one another. Another crewman practised changing into warm clothing as quickly as possible when he was in his cabin, so he would be prepared if his worst fears came true and the ship sank.

It was around midnight, going on January 16, and the ship was churning through heavy, seven-metre seas when an extremely loud bang rang out and the hull of the ship whipped fiercely like a child's skipping rope. Nothing came of it and the ship continued on her way. Then, shortly after 4 a.m., there was another huge bang and once again the hull whipped and vibrated severely. This time the general alarm went off. Everyone made their way to the afterdeck to discover that the ship had broken its back and was torn in two. The propeller was still turning, taking the ship in a slow circle. Suddenly, through the dark and driving snow, some of the crew could see the bow of a ship coming towards them. Salvation! A ship was close by that would rescue them! Their sudden elation and hopes turned to abject horror when they saw the name *Flare* on the bow — they realized they'd circled back to mistake their own bow as a rescue ship.

The crew needed to abandon immediately if they were to survive, but with a 30-degree list the starboard lifeboats were inaccessible. Moving to the port lifeboats, the crew realized the extra lashings that had been used to secure the boats against the heavy vibrations on the voyage now hampered their efforts to free them. The icy condition of the decks also made it difficult to launch the boats. Some crew members had managed to launch a life raft off the stern and secured it to the rail with a line, but when they went back, the line had chafed through and the life raft was lost. One of the crew was sent inside to make the hasty distress call before rushing back to abandon ship with the rest of them. The *Flare*'s crew was out of time and out of luck — the stern section sank within 30 minutes. Although the bow remained afloat, nobody had been in that part of the ship. For the crew of the *Flare*, a horrid night in a brutal sea would determine their fate. All the while, there were many people at work looking for them.

The MRSC in St. John's and RCC in Halifax were passing information back and forth as they received it. The *Stolt Aspiration* had arrived on position at 6:12 a.m. but found nothing, either visually or on radar — no radar targets indicating a ship and no sign of the flotsam or an oil slick that would indicate a sinking. The MRSC redirected the *Stolt Aspiration* to search another area between the two Mayday positions. The pale grey light of day was filtering through the solid overcast of clouds when the ship reached the new coordinates at 7:45 a.m. There was good visibility, but nothing was found. The end of Steve Waller's shift had come and gone, but it was so busy that the regional superintendent for search and rescue asked Steve if he could stay and help out. "It was really, really busy," Steve recalls. "I handed everything over to the coordinator coming on duty that morning and it was just swamped, so I stayed." He would end up staying until close to 7 p.m., pulling a 24-hour shift.

As daylight broke, King Air Rescue 01 was searching the original Mayday position while Hercules Rescue 306 was searching the Inmarsat position. The Labrador helicopter Rescue 303 had arrived on scene and was making an expanding square search of the original Mayday position. At 7:30 a.m., Labrador Rescue 304 in Sydney was brought into the picture.

*The Sinking of the* Flare

Tony Isaacs and Paul Jackman were search-and-rescue technicians who had finished a training mission the day before. Because of the weather they had ended up staying in Sydney overnight along with the flight crew of Labrador 304: pilot Captain Chris Brown, co-pilot Captain Richard Gough, and the flight engineer, Master Corporal Rob Butler. Search-and-rescue technicians (Sartechs) are specialists who occupy a unique niche in the search-and-rescue community. The training for a Sartech can be tough, but exhilarating. As Tony puts it, "The course ... is 10 months long and to be honest it was the most challenging and rewarding course that I ever did, and I think that most Sartechs would agree with me."

Aside from the obvious and necessary medical training, the trainees learn to parachute into a number of dicey situations, including night jumps, water jumps, and jumps into confined places. They also learn to SCUBA dive, to ice climb in the Athabaskan ice fields, to rock climb, and about arctic survival, helicopter operations, and ground search techniques. It's a military trade and a candidate must work in another related profession for four years before being accepted for the year-long training in Comox, British Columbia.

After they graduate, Sartechs join an operational unit and undergo on-the-job training that culminates in a demanding test before they can become a fully qualified team member. Tony Isaacs had been a Sartech since 1983, and with 15 years of experience, he was the senior of the two Sartechs and the team leader. He had been involved in more than a few hairy missions. On one such mission, Tony assisted in hoisting four people from a 13-metre fishing vessel that had lost its stabilizers and rudder to founder in 40-knot winds and 12-metre seas. "Add to this the fact that the captain was refusing to leave his boat until we rolled over almost 90 degrees, and then he couldn't get off quick enough!" recalls Tony.

Paul Jackman was fresh out of training and had only been in the position for a scant four months. His only major mission had been assisting in the rescue of survivors from the sinking bulk carrier *Vanessa*, 1,300 kilometres out in the Atlantic Ocean. "All I did was throw flares from the plane for what felt like eons," he says. "But when you're brand new in the trade, you feel like you've made a difference." Paul was looking forward to making his first real jump.

When they woke up at the hotel in Sydney on the morning of January 16, the weather was still terrible, with high winds and blowing snow. Paul remembers that the waves were still high and crashing on the shore. After breakfast and prior to heading to the airport for the flight back to Greenwood, pilot Chris Brown called RCC Halifax to check in. He was told of the incident that had occurred in the wee hours of the morning and informed that they were the closest resource and were being assigned to head to the scene.

Dashing out to the airport, the group fired up the helicopter and prepared to leave. Paul recalls that the wind was blowing so hard that snow was getting into the engine air intakes, which could create problems once the engines heated up. Sure enough, about 15 minutes into the flight they saw pinkish red fluid leaking toward the back of the helicopter and thought they had a leak of hydraulic fluid, which could have disastrous consequences. They called a Pan Pan — the international radio signal for an urgent broadcast, a step just below a Mayday — turned around, and headed back to Sydney. Meanwhile, being a rookie, Paul thought maybe he should examine the leak to see if something could be done. "I wanted to go check it out, but Tony threw me down into my seat and had me do up my seatbelt before landing," he recalls.

Tony was the veteran and recognized that if the helicopter lost power, it would be out of control; if Paul wasn't buckled in, he'd be thrown around the cabin like a tennis ball, potentially injuring himself or even being killed when the chopper suddenly decelerated on hitting the water. Once they landed, flight engineer Rob Butler found the problem and fixed it, and then once again they were on their way. It was 8:25 a.m., and it would be about two hours of flight time to the search site. Steve and the aeronautical coordinators at RCC had another resource on the way.

Steve Waller knew that time was against them. The longer the search took, the farther anything being affected by tides, current, and winds would drift from the distress site, which made for a constantly expanding search area. By 8 a.m. the initial Mayday site had turned up empty, and the focus began to shift to the site indicated by the Inmarsat distress, although nothing had been found up until that point. Hercules Rescue 306 and King Air Rescue 01 started expanding square searches from the midpoint between the two differing distress positions. The Hercules worked south and west of the position and the King Air worked north and east. The hope was that covering the area between the two distress positions would give a greater potential for success.

As King Air Rescue 01 was starting its search, the crew suddenly saw two surface targets on their radar. One was identified as the *Stolt Aspiration*; the other was unidentified. The unidentified target wasn't investigated immediately because of confusion between RCC and the aircraft involved in the search. The overcast conditions, snow squalls, and fog made for declining radio conditions and intermittent contact with RCC. "There was also some confusion in the information passed back to RCC on who had found what, and when and where and whether it had been looked at," Steve explains.

Aside from the confusion, one thing Steve had learned as an SAR coordinator was to be thorough and not to make assumptions. Normally, when an aircraft has an unidentified radar target during a search, they'll investigate it themselves. If they're unable to go low enough to get visual confirmation because of bad weather, a ship will be sent to investigate. Experience and training has taught those involved in SAR that confirmation is absolutely necessary because too often, when you've found something, it isn't what you're looking for.

Steve illustrates this problem with a scenario used as a teaching tool in SAR courses. During a search for a downed plane, a search aircraft reports they've found a downed plane. The pilots want to parachute in the Sartechs immediately to assist any survivors. What do you do? Those who are thorough — who plot the position and check their geographic information system — discover that it is an old crash site. Those who aren't thorough are later faced with a situation where a Hercules aircraft finds the real crash site but has no Sartechs to send in because they had already parachuted in to investigate an old crash site. SAR coordinators have learned not to jump to conclusions and risk frittering away resources or wasting valuable time. While the unconfirmed target made for some hope that it would prove to be substantial, the searchers had to wait until they had a clearer overall picture before they could pull ships or aircraft from other tasks to investigate what could be a fishing vessel that wasn't reporting to anyone.

The sheer volume of incoming information Steve was dealing with was taxing, and the method of logging was cumbersome. RCC had a clipboard that would be passed back and forth between the air and marine coordinators on which they would both pen their log entries. With MRSC St. John's involved and much duplicate message traffic, a lot of entries were late and the log became less linear and more abstract. Steve coped, but it was difficult to keep everything straight as several hundred entries and dozens of pages of information were added. (Today, RCC has a more efficient electronic log that everyone can access simultaneously as needed.)

Hercules Rescue 306 was at the Inmarsat position by 8:10 a.m. RCC had them drop two data marker buoys. These cylinders released little air bags when they hit the water to allow them to float with the current. The buoys transmitted telemetry on water temperature and current. One was configured to represent a life raft in the water; the other was configured to represent a person by releasing a little sea anchor to slow it down. The temperature readings would assist in calculating how long before an individual might succumb to hypothermia. The information on the ocean current allowed the searchers to calculate how far a raft or person would drift. Usually these drift plots are based on historical water current data for any part of the ocean, but it's best to use up-to-date information if at all possible for greater precision. As Steve puts it, "Using historical information we can say that for the past 50 years the current in this position has always done such and such. The buoy may indicate that today is different."

The most common use for these buoys is to mark a debris field. The buoys will float with the debris, making it easier to locate later if it can't be searched immediately because of poor weather or darkness. In this case, the search teams wanted precise information about what was happening with the current in order to further define the search area. They now had the majority of their air assets on scene, and the search was on in earnest.

By 9:30 a.m. the aircraft were running low on fuel and began to fly into St. Pierre to refuel. Just before the King Air Rescue 01 departed, the pilot called Hercules Rescue 306 and said they would check out the unidentified radar target on their way to St. Pierre. At 10:09 a.m., skimming low under the gloom of the cloud cover, they spotted the bow of the *Flare*, heaving in the ocean. This sighting was the first clue that anyone involved in the rescue had about the fate of the ship. If they were to find survivors, they had to move fast.

Following their mishap on takeoff, Labrador Rescue 304 was chopping in low and fast toward the area where RCC had requested they run some search lines toward St. Pierre. Paul Jackman was in the back of the helicopter getting dressed when he heard a lot of commotion over his headset. Flight engineer Rob Butler had spotted an oil slick! Frantically picking up the pace, he took off his headset to finish dressing, and by the time he had put it back on, he heard Tony saying they had spotted an overturned lifeboat and, what's more, they could see four people desperately clinging to it.

Looking down at the capsized lifeboat, Paul saw one of the wretched souls lift his arm weakly and wave. Paul and Tony knew these men would be hypothermic, and they were prepared for this probability with their well-packed medical kit. Each swell was overrunning the fragile little boat, so the first priority was to get the survivors out of the water, which was killing them with every tick of the clock. Tony turned to Paul and said, "Okay, Paul, we found these ones really quick.

I'm going to go down and get these four and you can get the next ones."

Paul's heart sank with those words. He was fired up to do his first hoist, but he recognized and deferred to Tony's wisdom and experience. As keen as he was, he realized that while Tony winched down, he could have everything ready for the survivors as they were brought on board. He started preparing the items they would need from the medical kit and clearing a viable workspace in the back of the helicopter.

With his wet suit, fins, and mask, Tony was ready to go. He was energized with anticipation, but not nervous. Although they had drilled the procedures for this type of rescue so often that it was second nature and every move was automatic, their minds were still occupied with the tasks they had to accomplish. Pilot Chris Brown settled the Labrador into a hover in the "rest position," about 16 metres off the surface of the water and about 16 metres to the side of the lifeboat. Hovering directly over the capsized lifeboat would risk the powerful downdraft of the rotors blowing the survivors from their flimsy and tenuous position on the boat. Instead, Tony had the difficult job of slowly winching himself into the bitter, freezing water and then swimming 16 metres to the lifeboat while still hooked up, dragging the heavy cable all the way. It was arduous, exhausting work fighting his way through the waves. And swimming through the viscous slick of oil coating the surface made it even trickier. The thick, greasy smell of diesel oil made breathing harder, but he pressed on. He'd trained for this job, and those men on the boat needed him right now.

Once he arrived, there was no time for triage to assess who needed to be lifted first. For the most part, the survivors were lethargic and unresponsive. Their vacant eyes seemed to look right through him.

The rescue collar, which resembles a horse collar, is an elliptic, padded strap that goes around a person's chest and under their armpits, making it possible to hoist them up to the door of the helicopter. Both the rescue collar and the Sartech are secured to the same hook at the end of the cable, which allows the Sartech to support and steady the person being hoisted. Once Tony and the first survivor were lifted to the door, Paul and Rob helped pull them in. Paul could see that both Tony and the victim were completely drenched in the bunker C oil that coated the surface of the ocean. The freezing water had its effect on Tony as well, sapping so much of his strength that there was a change in plans. "Paul, get dressed. After this, you're going down for the next one." Being young and keen, Paul was excited that he was finally getting his chance to go to work and prove his worth.

Tony brought up the second victim, and then Paul took his place on the cable. As he was being winched down he could see why Tony was drained, swimming through a greasy oil slick and fighting the four-metre seas. Once in the water, Paul gasped as cold shock hit; he had a tough few seconds getting his breath. Today, Sartechs use dry suits that are insulated against the cold when on an operation like this, but at the time they weren't available.

As he swam hard toward the overturned lifeboat, Paul realized it was covered in a crust of ice. He wondered how he was going to get up on it to work the rescue collar around one of the men clinging desperately to the ribs of the boat. This thought had no sooner crossed his mind when a wave lifted him up and flung him towards the boat. He was aboard with a single kick. Looking into their eyes, Paul could see that the two remaining survivors were in a world of pain. Grabbing the nearest man, he fitted the rescue collar on him. Just as he was about to give the go signal to Rob Butler, who was working the hoist, the other man clinging to the raft grabbed Paul's leg and wouldn't let go. Paul told him he was coming back, but it didn't have any effect — the poor man was beyond reason. It would have been horrible to be stuck in the freezing waters of the Atlantic for hours, but now he was going to be down there alone. Paul had to give a little kick to wrench his leg free and then they were ascending to the Labrador. Quickly winching back down, Paul retrieved the last man, who was the most hypothermic of all. Paul looked into his eyes and could see that nobody was home.

When they had all four victims in the helicopter there was no time to waste. They started cutting the drenched, oil-soaked clothes off them and wrapped them in blankets as the Labrador sliced through the air at top speed for St. Pierre. The entire operation had taken about 20 minutes. Ideally, the

best way to begin medical treatment or the warming proto-
col would be to give the survivors warm intravenous fluids
to warm them from the core out, but the team had neither
the equipment nor the time on the short flight to St. Pierre.
Paul was shocked at how little the survivors were wearing —
T-shirts, underwear, and socks for the most part. It was incredible that they had survived almost six hours in the Atlantic.

The last man Paul had hoisted was thrashing around
frantically, trying to grab at anything to hold on to. In his
delirium, he wasn't aware that he was now safe. His thrashing was endangering the others and creating huge problems
for the Sartechs. Tony looked at Paul and hollered, "Hand me
your jacket!" Without hesitation, Paul tossed his coat to Tony,
who used it to pin the man down as well as provide him with
some insulation to begin the warming process.

Surprisingly, within five minutes the survivors started
coming around. One of the men asked Paul for a cigarette.
Paul told him he didn't smoke, and gently suggested that
lighting a match might not be a good idea given the fact they
were covered in fuel oil.

During the 20-minute flight to St. Pierre, Paul and Tony
questioned the survivors about what had happened. In
hearing the story of the horror-filled morning, the Sartechs
learned that six men had been clinging to that lifeboat
originally, but a few hours earlier, two had succumbed to
hypothermia, slipped off, and drowned. It would later be discovered that one of these men had become entangled in the

lines underneath the lifeboat that had offered these survivors a frozen island in a brutal sea.

Once they arrived in St. Pierre, the local gendarmes took over and were extremely cooperative in getting the survivors to the hospital and taking care of the crew of Rescue 304. Paul and Tony showered to clean off the cloying fuel oil cling-ing to their skin. Then they changed their clothes and went to the hospital to see if they could learn any more details of what had happened on the *Flare*. They talked to the nurses and were shocked to learn that one of the men had a body temperature of 26.9°C — a normal body temperature is 37°C, and once a person's temperature drops below 25°C it's certain death. This knowledge left Paul awestruck that the four men had survived at all.

Yugoslavian crewman Petar Markovic told Paul and Tony that this voyage on the *Flare* had been his first trip to sea. He had a pocketknife with him, and in his broken English told them, "You know, I wasn't going to drown at sea. If I was out there another hour ..." he drew a finger across his throat, "... that's how I was going." It drove home the pain and terror the survivors had undergone while bobbing around in frozen isolation for those interminably long hours.

After talking to the survivors, the Sartechs returned to their Labrador at the airport. They were heading back out to the debris field to continue the search and felt optimis-tic that they would find more survivors. RCC tasked them with inspecting the bow of the *Flare* to see if anyone was aboard and to check if the lifeboats had been launched. Disappointingly, they wouldn't discover any more people. Once they inspected the bow and saw the lifeboats in their davits, their hopes dimmed — they realized there was no chance of finding more survivors.

Meanwhile, RCC was concentrating all their assets in the immediate area.

### The Debris Field

Once the bow had been found, Steve Waller realized the ship had suffered a catastrophic structural failure. It wasn't found very far from the Inmarsat position, about 20 kilometres away, and now the search area was vastly reduced — from 100 kilometres across to less than 10, and from 3,200 square kilometres to 80. With all the aircraft combing the right area, various bits of debris and flotsam were spotted and called in. The reports were coming in much faster now. Two more overturned lifeboats and two rafts were found. A huge oil slick, 16 kilometres long and almost five kilometres wide, marked the area of the debris field.

Steve felt a certain measure of relief now that the bow had been found, but he shifted mental gears once he started thinking about potential rescue. There is a distinct difference between "search" and "rescue" that poses a dichotomy within the SAR coordinator's mind. The search portion of an operation is more challenging intellectually, an exercise in problem solving with very little emotional resonance. The rescue portion is almost entirely emotional, and the SAR coordinator receives a very large, emotional boost when they've successfully found the ship or plane for which they've been searching and can now look to rescuing survivors. "You're so happy on getting the news that there are survivors and they're alive. Relieved they're alive and you've contributed to that," says Steve.

Steve was elated to hear of the successful rescue carried out by Labrador Rescue 304, but as the clock ticked away and no further survivors were found, the mood shifted. Everyone realized that the remaining search would be for bodies. Labrador Rescue 113 found a life raft covered in oil, but it held no survivors. The helicopter crew punctured the raft to sink it so nobody else would fruitlessly search the same life raft, and then they continued their search. Rescue Labrador 303 found 13 bodies in the oil slick. It managed to recover four of them, which were flown to St. Pierre. Labrador Rescue 113 also found four bodies, recovered them, and flew them to St. Pierre, but the fumes from the oil were making the air crews sick. Back at RCC Halifax, Steve discussed this problem with the air coordinators. They decided to use the aircraft to locate the bodies and direct the ships to the site to recover them. The crews on the ships could bring the bodies aboard and strip them of their oil-soaked clothing, which they could leave on deck where the fumes wouldn't create the problems they had in the enclosed space of the helicopters.

At around noon, the *W. G. George* had arrived from

Burgeo, and over the next four hours, its crew managed to recover four more bodies. Four hours after the *W. G. George*'s arrival, the HMCS *Montreal* was on scene. It became, in effect, a floating morgue, as recovered bodies were taken aboard for their sad, final trip to shore.

The *W. G. George*'s chief engineer, Dana Benoit, had gone to work that morning not anticipating anything out of the ordinary. Dana was the first to arrive at the cutter station that morning, at 7:45 a.m., and the phone was already ringing before he opened the door. MRSC St. John's passed him the information they had and told him to get under way as soon as possible for the distress site, which that was roughly 100 kilometres away. Once off the phone, Dana called the captain and other two crewmen to let them know what was going on; then he flashed up the powerful diesel engines on the 16-metre, self-righting cutter, unhooked the lines to the shore power, and prepared it to leave.

It was slower going than usual because of the choppy, three-metre seas. The cutter heaved its way over the waves, but it could only make half its top speed of 20 knots, so it took until early afternoon before it arrived and could begin its search. The coordinator at MRSC St. John's had told Dana the scope of the problem, so he knew that it was going to be a new experience and that it was going to be bad. "I kept telling myself, 'We're going to see dead bodies. We're going to see dead bodies. We're going to see dead bodies,' and after a while, I just went blank," Dana recalls.

Once the *W. G. George* arrived, it was into the debris field immediately and motoring around in a filthy, scummy oil slick. It came across the deflated life raft and overturned lifeboats. With no sign of life, the ship continued its grisly search. The captain was driving the boat; the other three men would recover the bodies using nothing but manpower. They would attempt to grapple them with gaffer hooks, pull them in, and manhandle them out of the freezing water and onto the deck. They put on their safety harnesses (so they wouldn't fall or be swept overboard into the rough seas) and went to work.

When they found the first body, Dana's heart fell. The captain manoeuvred in while the crew began pulling him aboard. As they were taking him over the side, Dana told himself, "His family is going to be glad that his body has been recovered." The bitter pill of their dark and painful task just dissolved and left him as he continued his work. Frozen solid, the way each body was suspended in the water was the way it was brought aboard. Seeing how each body was dressed, Dana realized that the disaster had happened extremely fast. "They were clad pretty scantily," he explains. "One poor soul in particular had a pair of track pants, no shirt, no socks, that's it. So they put their life jackets on in total haste."

It was difficult work, especially given the rough sea conditions. Dana recalls that they were shipping water as swells broke over the side while they were manoeuvring to pick up the bodies. The four they recovered were transferred to the HMCS *Montreal* when it arrived on the scene.

## The Sinking of the Flare

In a curious turn of events, the first crew manning the Zodiac sent from the *Montreal* to transfer the bodies from the *W. G. George* had to turn back. One of the men aboard the Zodiac, a burly, strapping man, became spooked at the thought of the corpses and started screaming for them to take him back. They had to go back to get another crewman to make the transfer. Dana remembers that this scared him more than anything else.

The men on the *W. G. George* found another body under a lifeboat that they couldn't recover. They placed a data marker buoy there and later the HMCS *Montreal* recovered that body. Everything was completely contaminated with bunker C fuel oil. At one point the HMCS *Montreal* had sent a Zodiac over with trays of food for the crew of the *W.G. George*, but nobody had any appetite, and when one man saw the food he threw up over the side of the boat. The oil was all over them, from head to foot; it had even gotten under the collars of their survival suits and down their necks. The captain was the only one spared from this particularly unpleasant consequence of their task.

When the transfers were complete, the *W. G. George* was released and headed to Fortune, Newfoundland. Once they arrived in Fortune the next morning, the crew cleaned up, had breakfast, and then headed back to their motel rooms to get some sleep. Dana realized this operation had perhaps had more effect on him than he'd thought when he couldn't get the key to his room in the lock. He was shaking too hard.

Meanwhile, the *W. G. George* had to be blasted with steam to decontaminate it and clean off the oil. The other Coast Guard cutter on the scene, the *W. Jackman*, fared better but still had a grim task.

Captain Chris Whelan aboard the *W. Jackman* had been tasked later than the *W. G. George* and had farther to go — almost 144 kilometres. Therefore, this second cutter arrived much later. Chris was around 50 kilometres from the scene and encountering rough seas that reduced his speed when MRSC St. John's contacted him to change his orders. He was to head to St. Pierre to pick up the remains of those who had been recovered by the aircraft and transfer them to the HMCS *Montreal*. When the *W. Jackman* arrived in St. Pierre it was too late in the evening to do anything, so the local officials magnanimously arranged accommodations for the crew at a hotel — Canada and France have agreements in place for these kinds of situations.

The next morning, they loaded the remains aboard the *W. Jackman* for the trip to the *Montreal*. Given the sombre nature of the task, bureaucratic red tape was kept to a minimum. The gendarmes gave Chris all the documentation he would require for the release and transfer of the bodies to Canadian authorities. The remains had been put in clean body bags and wrapped in a tarpaulin, which would be lashed to the deck of the *W. Jackman* for the trip home. Despite these preparations, Chris could still see oil oozing out of the body bags and seeping through the tarpaulin.

## The Sinking of the Flare

As it turned out, the seas were too rough to make the transfer, so the *W. Jackman* ended up diverting to Fortune, where the Royal Canadian Mounted Police (RCMP) arranged for hearses to take the remains to local funeral homes.

\* \* \*

The search was winding down by 5 p.m. on January 16. Fourteen bodies had been recovered, but there were seven still missing. Shortly after that, the search was called off, with 15 bodies recovered but no more survivors. An exhausted Steve Waller was finally relieved from his post. On his way home he pondered what had happened that day, working through it in his mind. Because he often deals with situations that can result in unhappy conclusions, his approach has become pragmatic: he keeps his work and home life separate. "I'm not 100 percent successful, but I try to keep them separate so when I walk through the door, I don't want to start talking about the death and destruction of the day," he explains.

He doesn't second-guess himself because it's an exercise in futility. Rather, he takes solace in the fact that he's done the job to the very best of his ability and will continue to do so — as do all those who labour to make the inherently dangerous job of plying the world's oceans.

After Ann-Margret arrived home from work that morning, she slept until noon. When she awoke, she turned on the television, and the *Flare* was the top Canadian news story. She watched in disbelief as she learned the full scope of the tragedy. Looking back now, she realizes that this incident was a defining moment in her career. "It reminds you exactly what you're there for. So many shifts pass by quietly. I now appreciate my job more, as well as the work we do. You can get into a rut with mundane tasks; an incident like this drives home the importance of the job," she says.

The bow of the *Flare* stayed afloat for four and a half days, drifting steadily south until if finally sank approximately 160 kilometres north of Sable Island. While it was adrift, it was a hazard to shipping, and a notice was broadcast by Coast Guard radio stations to keep ships aware of the bow's position. While it was adrift, photographs were taken of the bow. The photos were used by Transport Canada safety inspectors to figure out what happened to cause the *Flare* to sink. Along with the photographs, they also had video that had been taken of both bow and stern from a remote-controlled submersible operated from the Coast Guard ship *Earl Grey* six months after the sinking. With this evidence, and with records of past inspections of the ship, their findings indicated that the steel in the *Flare* had become very brittle, leaving it susceptible to fracture. From the photographs of the bow, there was evidence that the ship had been improperly ballasted; it rode too high in the rough seas, which allowed the hull to flex too much given the forces of nature that were pummelling it during its voyage. The hull repeatedly bent like a tree in a high wind, stressing the brittle steel of the hull until the ship broke its back, splitting in two and putting its crew in dire and deadly straits.

Paul Jackman is now a team leader who remembers and preaches the lessons he learned from Tony Isaacs so many years ago. He also has vivid recollections of his first big rescue and keeps a scrapbook full of articles and memorabilia from the various rescues he's been involved with over the years. One of the items in his scrapbook is a copy of a letter he received from survivor Petar Markovic, which Petar composed and mailed — along with photographs of the Markovic family — after he arrived home from his harrowing journey. Petar's English is a little rough at times, but from this excerpt, there is no mistaking the grateful spirit in which the letter was written:

> *Dear Saviours,*
> *This letter written to you is one of the most difficult letters I have ever written. I simply can't find the words to express my gratitude for everything you did for me. I believe in God and in fate and I hope you'll be rewarded for your good deeds and therefore I wish all of you the best in your future life. When I speak about you I usually say that even the best movie director can't show on scene the absolute courage, skill and equipment that you possess. I am perfectly aware of the fact that you saved*

*my life twice. The first time rescuing me from the freezing water, the second time in the helicopter giving me first aid. I only have one objection. The cigarette (I am only kidding of course).*

Petar Markovic

# Glossary

**After, aft-:** Toward the rear or stern of a ship

**Ballast:** Additional weight to maintain a ship's stability. A ship empty of cargo rides too high in the water and takes on sea water in ballast tanks so it will ride lower for a smoother, more stable ride.

**Bulkhead:** A wall that crosses the hull and divides it into sections

**Cantilever:** A projecting structure, such as a beam or platform, that is supported at one end and carries a load at the other end.

**COSPAS-SARSAT:** Search and rescue satellite system

**Coxswain:** The person who steers a small boat

**Downflooding:** Sea water entering the vessel's hull by way of non-watertight hatches and decks

**Ecareg:** Eastern Canada Vessel Traffic Services Zone Regulations and its enforcing agency

**EPIRB:** Emergency position indicating radio beacon

**ETA:** Estimated time of arrival

**Forward, fore-:** Towards the front, or bow of a ship

**GPS:** Global position system and its related satellites

**Heaving:** The up and down motion on the vertical axis of a ship at sea

**HF radio:** High frequency, long-range radio with almost unlimited range depending on the power source and conditions

**Inmarsat:** International Maritimes Satellite system

**Knot:** The standard maritime measurement for velocity. One knot equals one nautical mile per hour, or 1.85 kilometres per hour. In ancient times, ships would measure their speed by tossing a rope with a log attached overboard. Then, by measuring the length of rope pulled away from the ship in a given amount of time, they could tell their speed. Eventually, rather than measuring the rope, they just tied knots in it at regular intervals and counted how many knots went out in the set time, hence the term.

**List:** A continuous leaning to one side

**Mayday:** An emergency in which a ship is in grave and imminent danger

**Mayday relay:** After receiving a Mayday call, the shore station will repeat the message on the distress and calling frequencies. The shore station has a more powerful transmitter with greater range, which increases the probability of a response from ships in a position to assist.

**Medium frequency (MF) radio:** MF Radio with a range of 250–500 kilometres, depending on conditions. At night the range can extend immeasurably. Your car's AM radio is MF — during the day it picks up local stations, but if you tune along the dial at night you will hear stations thousands of kilometres away.

**MRSC:** Marine rescue sub-centre. An adjunct to the RCC, it is a regional office that coordinates rescues in other Coast Guard regions for the RCC.

**Pan Pan:** An urgent situation one step removed from a Mayday. The words "Pan Pan" are repeated three times to alert those listening to the radio that an urgent broadcast is about to be made.

**Pitching:** The seesaw motion of a ship taking waves on the bow or the stern

**Port:** The left side of a ship

**Rescue Coordination Center (RCC):** A network of regional offices that control and coordinate all ships, aircraft, and ground crews during a rescue effort in their area

**Rolling:** The side to side rocking motion of a ship with waves hitting on port or starboard

**SAR:** Search and rescue

**Sartech:** Search and rescue technician

**Shipping water:** Taking on water that comes over the side of the ship from boarding seas

**Shoals:** A hidden sandbar or rising bottom that forms a shallow place, which is a danger to navigation

**Starboard:** The right side of a ship

**Sumps:** A hole or depression that is the mouth of a pump intake

**Superstructure:** The portion of a ship that rises above the main deck like a building and houses interior workspaces and accommodations

**Thrusters:** Small engines with propellers, located in tunnels on the sides of a vessel, that are used to control lateral movement

**Universal Time Coordinated (UTC):** Because ships are constantly moving, the commercial shipping world as well as the military use UTC as a standard time for everyone no matter where they are located. UTC corresponds to Greenwich Mean Time, which is the time zone at 0 degrees longitude that runs directly through Greenwich, England. UTC times are often given as three number pairs — the first two are the day, then the hour, then the minute.

**Very high frequency (VHF) radio:** a line-of-sight range of 80–120 kilometres; Your car's FM radio is VHF.

**Wheelhouse:** The bridge or room from which the ship is controlled; The helm, or wheel controlling the rudder as well as engine and navigational controls are located there.

**Zodiac:** A small, semi-rigid boat with inflated pontoons and an outboard motor

# Further Reading

Beeby, Dean. *Deadly Frontiers.* Fredericton, NB: Goose Lane Editions, 2001.

House, J.D. (John Douglas). *But Who Cares Now?: The Tragedy of the Ocean Ranger.* St. John's, Nfld: Breakwater Books, 1987.

# Acknowledgments

First of all, I would like to thank everyone I interviewed in respect to each of these three incidents for their participation and assistance. These stories are theirs; I am merely a scribe. During their recollections, they had me on the edge of my seat, anxious to learn what happened next.

Peter Fraser, Scott Clements, and Dave Lever were extremely helpful in recalling their roles during the blowout on the *Vinland*. I'd like to additionally thank Dave for the insight he offered into the broader world of search and rescue, a subject he knows intimately since he left the life at sea to work as a maritime coordinator at RCC Halifax. The information he offered on the effects of hypothermia and cold shock gave me a greater understanding of the dangers faced by those who ply the world's unforgiving oceans.

I'd like to thank Clinton Cariou and Jeff Cox for their compelling and dramatic recounting of the sinking of the *Rowan Gorilla 1*. Clinton offered me a quick, general, yet surprisingly comprehensive education about how an oil rig functions and how these mechanical leviathans are transported across the vastness of the ocean. Jeff filled in many details about being responsible for an $80-million vessel and his thoughts and reactions during the storm. I'd also like to thank Wayne Decoste for confirming additional details of what occurred during this incident.

To Steve Waller, Ann-Margret White, Tony Isaacs, Paul Jackman, Dana Benoit, and Chris Whelan, I offer my heartfelt gratitude and appreciation for giving me a clear, overall picture of how a search-and-rescue operation proceeds from the perspective of the rescuers. Steve's extensive insights into his internal process, as well as the solid perspective he gave me of how the SAR system functions, were invaluable. Paul and Tony provided me with a glimpse into the life and mindset of a Sartech, which gave me a greater respect and admiration for the tough job these "saviours of the sea" endure. I'd also like to thank Peter Bartlett for tolerating my incessant questions on satellite systems and the knowledge he offered in that area.

My sources for confirming the chronologies and certain details within the accounts were indispensable. For the *Vinland* incident, I referred to the COGLA "Report of Investigation of Events Culminating in a Blowout of Gas and Condesate at Shell ET A1 Uniacke G-72." Thank you to J. D. Roche, the archivist at the Canada–Nova Scotia Offshore Petroleum Board, for her assistance in finding and making this report available. For the *Rowan Gorilla 1* incident, I used "Marine Casualty Report on the Capsizing and Sinking of MODU *Rowan Gorilla 1*. USCG 16732/02 HQS 92," which I found on the U.S. Coast Guard website. For events involving the *Flare*, I relied on "Canadian Transportation Safety Board Report Number M98N0001, Marine Investigation Report.

## Acknowlegments

Break-Up and Sinking the Bulk Carrier 'FLARE' Cabot Strait 16 January 1998," which was available on their website.

I'd like to thank my good friend Joyce Glasner for her help in a number of areas. First and foremost, for offering encouragement and the occasional kick in the pants, which motivated me to lift myself from the world of the dilettante to that of a committed writer. I'd like to thank her for reading the manuscript and offering suggestions on strengthening the narrative and for her education on the process of becoming an author. To Kara Turner, Jill Foran, and Lee Craig at Altitude Publishing, I'd like to offer my heartfelt thanks for their help in shaping the manuscript and giving me the opportunity to tell these stories. I'd also like to thank Bill Lamont (my go-to grammar guy), Don Dupuis, and Peter Bartlett for reading the manuscript and offering advice about how to make it stronger. Paul Kendrick at RCC also offered information in respect to resources, which I much appreciate. Rhea Porter, Regis Verner, Lisa Carson, and Larry Wilson offered their assistance along the way to make this book possible.

Finally, I'd like to thank my wife Joanne for reading the manuscript and giving me her thoughts, as well as our four children, Kristiane, Kristopher, Michael, and Michelle, for their infinite patience and support while their dad was tying up the computer. It was much appreciated. This book would not have been possible without my family's encouragement and support.

# Photo Credits

# Author's Biography

Mark Chatham is a Marine Communications and Traffic Services (MCTS) officer with the Canadian Coast Guard at MCTS Halifax. He is also a freelance writer. He lives in Dartmouth with his wife Joanne, their four children, and their Wheaten terrier, Sanchez.

# Amazing Author
# Question and Answer

## What was your inspiration for writing *Rescues on the High Seas*?

Ever since I was a child I've been fascinated by the ocean. It's compelling and it's also somewhat frightening in a primal sense. I think it's amazing that a large number of people make their living on the ocean, given its mercurial nature and the inherent dangers. Something which I find admirable is how people can risk their lives to save others when the seas turn lethal in harsh weather. A lot of people are involved any time there's a marine incident: radio operators, the Rescue Co-ordination Center, pilots, other mariners, and others too numerous to mention. I wanted to convey the dynamic of a marine rescue and give an overview from various perspectives of those involved.

## What surprised you most while you were conducting your research?

The fact that no matter how desperate the situation for those in immediate danger, a command structure and complete co-operation were always maintained. Those involved didn't fall to pieces despite the intensity of the stress and the fact that they were constantly being hit by deteriorating conditions and radical, detrimental changes in the situation which complicated measures they were taking to save themselves.

## What do you most admire about the people in this Amazing Story?

Their utter professionalism and dedication to doing their jobs, as well as their ability to think on their feet.

## Which escapade in the book do you most identify with?

As I'm a professional radio operator, most definitely Scott Clements or Ann-Margret's experiences taking the Mayday calls. I've experienced a situation similar to that of Ann-Margret's in which there was a snap call and I was unable to maintain contact with the vessel, although this was due to poor radio conditions rather than the vessel sinking. Fortunately, in that particular case, there was a yacht that had heard the initial call and could relay the information for me.

## Did you run into any difficulties while researching the book?

Finding the proper individuals to interview was somewhat problematic. It's been at least a decade since the latest of these incidents occurred and in many cases it took some detective work to locate those involved.

## What part of the writing process did you enjoy most?

Definitely the interviews! I was on the edge of my seat during the live interviews by phone or in person. My method during these interviews seemed to be a probative question then a lot of: "Then what happened? Yikes! Then what happened next? Wow!" It truly was compelling and these people had amazing stories to tell. I was necessarily more restrained in email queries, but read the responses with intense interest.

## Why did you become a writer? Who inspired you?

I have an artistic sensibility that I've indulged through both music and painting — writing seemed to be the next logical step. I've always been a voracious reader of both fiction and non-fiction. There are a number of authors who inspired me to write. From classical writers such as Charles Dickens, John Steinbeck, and William Faulkner to more contemporary influences like Stephen King, John Irving, and Margaret Atwood.

## Who are your Canadian heroes?

Pierre Trudeau, Tommy Douglas, and Margaret Atwood to name a few celebrities. The true heroes are those who give themselves selflessly to help others.

## Which other Amazing Stories would you recommend?

*The Halifax Explosion* by Joyce Glasner is a comprehensive, exciting, and page-turning rendering of what happened in Halifax Harbour over a 24-hour period of that terrible day. Sandra Phinney's *Risk Taker's and Innovators* is a delightful read, detailing a number of Canadian inventors and entrepreneurs. I was surprised at some of the innovations we commonly use, all of which were developed by Canadians.

AMAZING STORIES™

# THE HALIFAX EXPLOSION

Surviving the Blast that Shook a Nation

HISTORY/HUMAN INTEREST

by Joyce Glasner

# THE HALIFAX EXPLOSION
## Surviving the Blast that Shook a Nation

*"Suddenly, a terrible blast jolted Andrew Cobb
out of his reverie. It felt as though a giant hand
had smacked the train, tipping it up at
a precarious angle before dropping
it back to the tracks with a crash."*

A boat full of explosives heads in to the harbour
as a large cargo ship steams out to sea. What happened next, on a fateful day in December 1917, is
etched in history. At least 1900 people lost their
lives and 9000 were injured when the largest
man-made explosion ever experienced ripped
through Halifax and nearby Dartmouth. Panic
reigned as the survivors struggled to compre-
hend what had happened.

 True stories. Truly Canadian.

ISBN 1-55153-942-X

AMAZING STORIES™

# D-DAY

Canadian Heroes of the
Famous World War II Invasion

HISTORY/MILITARY

by Tom Douglas

# D-DAY
## Canadian Heroes of the Famous World War II Invasion

*"As the Canadian armour neared the highway, Meyer yelled 'Attack!' and all hell broke loose."*

On June 6, 1944, a daring and ambitious invasion of Europe changed the course of World War II, eventually leading to the surrender of Nazi Germany. During the night, through storms and high seas, the Allied forces swept towards the beaches of Normandy in France. This is the story of the bravery, the heroism, and the sheer dumb luck of the more than 14,000 Canadians who played a crucial role in that incredible event.

 True stories. Truly Canadian.

ISBN 1-55153-795-8

# WEST COAST ADVENTURES
## Shipwrecks, Lighthouses, and Rescues Along Canada's West Coast

*"... The ship began to break up almost
at once and the women and children
were lashed to the rigging above the reach
of the sea. It was a pitiful sight to see
frail women, wearing only night dresses,...
trying to shield children in their arms."*
Crewman of the *Valencia*

The southwest coast of Vancouver Island is a reef-studded stretch, notorious for dramatic winter storms and thick cloaks of summer fog. Many ships have found themselves well off course, even lost, during sudden storms. This book tells the stories of the sailors, lighthouse keepers, and linemen who have weathered these west coast storms.

 True stories. Truly Canadian.

ISBN 1-55153-990-X

# RESCUE DOGS
## Crime and Rescue Canines
## in the Canadian Rockies

*"Sam [the rescue dog] was so eager that when the day came to get back on a snowmobile, he didn't hesitate. We drove off to another avalanche exercise while he sat on the seat in front of me, where I could keep an eye on him, barking his approval to one and all as we headed up the mountain."*

Dale Portman's insightful storytelling is a heartwarming affirmation of the bond between man and dog. This collection of crime and rescue stories highlights the vital role dogs play in saving lives, upholding the law, and recovering bodies. Dale's adventures with Sam, a German Shepherd, and the escapades of Ginger and the other working dogs featured in this book make a fascinating read.

 True stories. Truly Canadian.

ISBN 1-55153-995-0

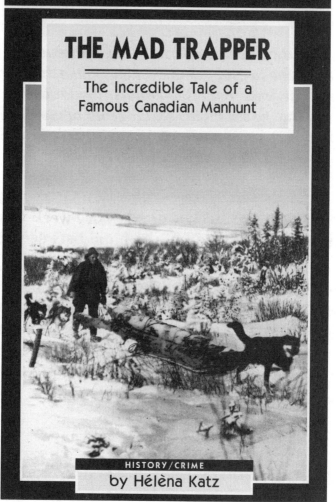

AMAZING STORIES™

# THE MAD TRAPPER

The Incredible Tale of a
Famous Canadian Manhunt

HISTORY/CRIME
by Hélèna Katz